In
Sickness
and in
Health

In Sickness and in Health

Health

*LOVE STORIES FROM THE
FRONT LINES OF AMERICA'S
CAREGIVING CRISIS*

LAURA MAULDIN

ecco
An Imprint of HarperCollins*Publishers*

IN SICKNESS AND IN HEALTH. Copyright © 2026 by Laura Mauldin. All rights reserved. No part of this book may be used or reproduced in any manner whatsoever without written permission except in the case of brief quotations embodied in critical articles and reviews. For information, address HarperCollins Publishers, 195 Broadway, New York, NY 10007. In Europe, HarperCollins Publishers, Macken House, 39/40 Mayor Street Upper, Dublin 1, D01 C9W8, Ireland.

HarperCollins books may be purchased for educational, business, or sales promotional use. For information, please email the Special Markets Department at SPsales@harpercollins.com.

Ecco® and HarperCollins® are trademarks of HarperCollins Publishers.

hc.com

FIRST EDITION

Designed by Alison Bloomer

Library of Congress Cataloging-in-Publication Data has been applied for.

ISBN 978-0-06-333913-2

Printed in the United States of America

25 26 27 28 29 LBC 5 4 3 2 1

We caused the problems: then we sat and
watched as they grew into crises.
—OCTAVIA BUTLER, *PARABLE OF THE TALENTS*

When I say "I love you," it means that I want to be near
the feeling of ambivalence our relation induces and hope
that what's negative, aggressive, or just hard about it
doesn't defeat what's great about it . . . We cannot know
each other without being inconvenient to each other.
—LAUREN BERLANT, *ON THE INCONVENIENCE OF OTHER PEOPLE*

Contents

Author's Note

This book is a work of nonfiction, featuring my own story as well as the true stories of others across the country. Many of the people I interviewed for this book worked patiently with me over a period of nearly five years, answering my calls and inviting me to visit with them. They were generous collaborators, allowing me to fact check details as we went. The events and experiences detailed herein have been rendered faithfully, as told to me by them, to the best of my abilities. Others have also read this book to ensure the accuracy of these accounts. To protect their privacy while retaining the integrity of their stories, some names and identifying circumstances have been changed.

Into the Fog

THE FIRST TIME I MET J WAS ON A CEMENT-BAKING AUGUST afternoon, as I sat sweating on the steps of Madison Square Garden. It was 2005, I was twenty-seven years old, and I had just moved to New York City. I was lingering at the top of the steps with a couple of friends I'd known through the queer community back in Austin, friends who had welcomed me to the city by inviting me to watch a WNBA game with them. Now we were waiting, waiting because one of my friends had said to hold on, there was still one last person to arrive.

I was squinting into the sun when I caught sight of a woman walking across the plaza from the subway toward us. She was taller than me, and, in my just-arrived sensibilities, she seemed to embody a kind of New York City confidence that I felt immediately awed by. J strutted up the steps wearing yellow Nike high-tops, her brown hair piled high in a men's-style pompadour, and I was practically in love before she reached the top step.

I spent the whole game trying to make conversation with her, lightly touching her shoulder, having finagled my way into sitting next to her. When she told me she was a chef, I went on and on about this salad dressing I liked to make. She humored me; she was actually a pastry chef. Her specialty was chocolate, and she told me about working as a food stylist for magazines and on an ad campaign for a high-end chocolate company. J was magnanimous and charming with everyone. And I was falling all over myself trying to get her undivided attention.

I was so singularly focused on her the whole time that I don't even remember the game, who won or who lost. We all departed the venue together. I kept talking to her on the subway too. I was also new to the subway, but she seemed so comfortable, standing nonchalantly with one arm hanging from the subway pole above her head. As we approached the Fourteenth Street station, I wished I didn't have to transfer to another train to get home. I exited onto the platform, turning to catch another glimpse of her through the window. She was still talking with our other friends, but meeting my eyes, she lifted her free hand up at me in a casual wave.

———

It wasn't until December that I ran into her again, dancing at a lesbian bar in Brooklyn. The dance floor was a dimly lit mesh of bodies, faceless and drifting past—except for her. There she was: the signature pompadour, the seductive confidence. J was standing off to the side, surveying the room. My breath caught. We made eye contact; she smiled and waved. *She remembers me!* I thought giddily. She made her way to me and suddenly we were moving in sync, as if caught in each other's gravity. I became aware that the thing I had dreamed of might finally be happening. Since meeting her that day in August, I'd started my graduate program in sociology, gotten a first semester under my belt, and had been running around making new friends— finding different queer events to go to, expanding my circle, trying to mitigate the loneliness that comes with being new in town, and to New York City in particular. But J had always been in the back of my mind, and I'd wondered if I'd get to see her again. Now while we danced, she finally beamed her attention on me, and it was as if we were the only people in the room.

Moments later she nodded her head toward the bar, raised an eyebrow. We walked off the dance floor to get drinks and find a place to talk. Cocktails in hand, I did my best to be interesting and cute, to impress her. And after long conversations and batting lashes on my part, she kissed me. Any embarrassment I had floated away with the sheer lightning she sent through my body. I was no longer aware of anything around me; the noise and darkness of the bar suddenly shifted, replaced with a kind of brute physical attraction that pulsed with possibility, a possibility that was at once sexual and romantic, but also felt like home.

Over the next several weeks, I succumbed to the irrepressible need to run, not walk, the whole way to her apartment. In her kitchen, she would tell me that to get a job in a fancy restaurant, sometimes applicants were asked to simply cook an egg. She'd pull down her enormous white binders of recipes from culinary school and talk to me about the flavor profiles of some of her favorite cookies, Earl Grey or bourbon pecan. J also kept a list of restaurants, organized by neighborhood, that she was constantly adding to. When she found ones that were reliably good, she would add them to a small piece of paper, folded up in her wallet for reference. She was like magic: wherever we were, she would consult it to conjure the best meal in the world.

That winter, we mailed love letters to each other, though we both lived in Brooklyn. In January, she wrote: *It is Sunday morning. . . . As I was drifting into slumber, I felt your fingertips on my collarbone. And I was wishing I could wrap my legs around your body.* A few days later, I received another letter: *Laura, it's been an absolute pleasure and I am smitten.*

One evening, she visited my aunt's apartment, where I lived at the time. It was across the street from the enormous and foreboding building that houses the Brooklyn Museum of Art. On that night, the museum was swelling up from the street, surrounded by heavy fog, its edges smudged and gray. J loved architecture and told me about the building's features and the architectural firm that built it. *McKim, Mead & White, neoclassical.* We were mesmerized by the sight of it, neither of us had ever seen it look like this before, shrouded in such thick fog. We decided to take my dog and set out on a walk to investigate, to move closer into the fog.

As we walked on the wide sidewalk in front of the museum, we linked arms in the cold. We stopped to gaze up at it, our eyes following the columns all the way to the top until the fog smudged it out of existence. *Was it really there?* we wondered. Were we witnessing some great architectural ghost? We thought it was eyeing us, watching us. We made our way down the street to the meadow in Prospect Park and quickly realized how dark and foggy it was there too. We could hardly see anything. I was frightened, but I felt safer with J, standing there in her brown puffy coat and black knit hat, looking at me with wonder. Her hands hung from her coat, ungloved, and I thought to myself that her hands were the most perfect hands I had ever held.

A couple of months later, she left town for a few days and I, deep in my infatuation, felt like my heart was being crushed under the weight of her absence. The day she returned was a bitterly cold Valentine's Day. By then, I had moved to her neighborhood, so I made my way across Williamsburg to her apartment, as giddy as an adolescent. I strolled past the neighborhood place we thought had the best burgers. I passed the bodega that I had made up a silly jingle for when we were get-ting late-night sandwiches there after hanging out at the gay bar around the corner.

Then, in the cold shade of the Brooklyn-Queens Express-way, cars whirring above me on the arc of the overpass, I thought of her body: the way her slender fingers looked when they were slack, the shape of her eyes, her strong jaw, and how she threw her head back when she laughed. And maybe it was something I had heard in her voice when she'd called to ask me over, but as the wind kicked up, I was troubled by a diffuse sorrow. I dismissed it as a feature of my romantic side, brought on by the stark contrast of the bleak winter cityscape and the heat of my anticipation. I furrowed my brow and pushed the feeling away.

When I arrived at her apartment, I was all desire. She opened the door wearing my favorite sweater of hers—black-and-brown striped with a black lightning bolt woven just above her heart—and she smelled of white musk. I stripped off my winter coat and breathlessly told her how much I had missed her. I wanted to wrap myself around her, but she seemed trou-bled, aloof.

We settled in and sat down to face each other on her living-room floor, lit by the warm glow of a single lamp, her large brown eyes staring into mine. She said she had something to tell me but that she was afraid. I reached for her hand to still her trembling, telling her sweetly, honestly, naively, that it would be okay, whatever it was, that we would be okay.

"My leukemia is back," she told me. My heart sank. A couple of weeks earlier, she had been experiencing pain in her right shin. She had mentioned having leukemia, a blood cancer, a few years before, but told me she was in remission and doing just fine. I had thought nothing of her going to the doctor recently to assess some shin pain. But the doctor had biopsied the painful spot on her tibia and the pathology report showed that her leukemia had shown up in her bones.

Suddenly she was telling me that if she was to have any hope of staying alive she would have to have a bone marrow transplant. If this didn't work, the disease would kill her. There was nothing else the doctors had that could possibly save her; all her other options had been exhausted with her previous treatments.

After losing both her parents, after making it through a previous round of leukemia treatments, she was facing death once again. And here we were, new lovers. I had already planned to give my heart to her piece by piece, but instead I would open myself up as wide as I could, all at once. It was simple, really. I was in love with her. I squeezed her hands and told her, "We will get through it."

———

The first time I visited J in the hospital was in March 2006. I rode the 6 train uptown by myself. Once inside the hospital, I got lost. The hallways were strange and labyrinthine; machine beeps echoed out in the corridors, bouncing off the white drop-ceiling tiles. I went through door after door, and when I finally found her, she was sitting like an abandoned child, alone in the corner of a dim room, wearing a gray wool hat and a hospital gown.

We locked eyes from the doorway. "Bear!" she exclaimed, one of her many nicknames for me. Setting my jaw, as I would so many more times in the coming years, I stepped in. I was shaking as I crossed toward her.

It had only been a couple of weeks since she told me about

her leukemia relapse, and in that sterile hospital room, our bodies responded immediately to each other, a chemical reminder that our romance was still new. She was full of IV-bag poison and the hormonal circulations of sorrow and fear. I was full of cortisol and naivete, swimming in adrenaline. We soaked in each other's pheromones, waded through sick liquids, and tried to find a current. We were each other's most powerful drug; conduits of dopamine and norepinephrine tunneled between us. We rode the high.

Our romance was not just a kind of euphoria, but also— or so we believed—an antidote. Falling in love felt like an all-powerful escape hatch from fear or tragedy. Whispering together in bed, days before she had checked into the hospital, we resolved that our love was a fantastical neutralizing agent. It would surely save us from what was happening to her; the universe could never be so cruel, we thought. In the wake of her diagnosis, we professed our love in the face of death, as though romance alone was some kind of protection from it.

She had chosen me, and I her. There was a specialness conveyed in that choosing. Somewhere inside me, I understood that the specialness was supposed to fuel my care for her, to provide me a boundless well to draw from. If my love for her was bottomless, a renewable resource, then my capacity to care for her should be too; I should be able to endure whatever was coming.

From our early days onward then, I swore to bring the full force of my love and my labor to every matter that arose. All we needed was each other. I believed in our love. I believed in my capacity—after all, I had been chosen. I was the one.

The One

ONCE UPON A TIME, I MOVED TO NEW YORK AND FELL IN LOVE with J. But the story doesn't end there. For the next nearly five years, I was J's person. And though our relationship indeed had many hallmarks of a modern romance—getting an apartment together, making sweets every year for the holidays, eating our way through New York—over the years it became increasingly punctuated by harrowing visits to the ER, IV drips, incapacitating pain, and endless piles of pills. My romantic fairy tale had somehow turned into a living nightmare.

Without knowing it and without ever really having consented, I was demoted over time from lover to life-support system. I went from occupying the role of J's ideal romantic partner to being tasked with the complex, long-term job of keeping J alive. It was a disorienting role shift, swift in some ways and gradual in others. My demotion began as J's body weakened, and without any viable options for help with long-term home care, the demands on me steadily increased. What started as managing medications and appointments turned into showering and dressing her, swabbing her dry mouth and toileting her. Later, I learned to do many other highly specialized skills, like giving her IV infusions and performing daily physical therapy exercises. I learned that wondrous medical capabilities keep people alive, but only in a highly managed state—and that I would be the one doing most of the managing. I learned that the United States does not have adequate social safety nets for disabled people, leaving J and me to figure it out largely on our own.

Throughout it all, I lived with constant guilt anytime I left J at home alone to go to work, to study, to see a friend. Despite being with the person I loved, I was deeply lonely. It felt as though the rest of the world was going by, while I was trapped behind a two-way mirror. My graduate school classmates didn't know I spent nights on the floor of the emergency department of Memorial Sloan Kettering. My friends didn't know what it was like to live in daily fear. We had help from her best friend's family and others, but even this couldn't take away my loneliness. It was profound and painful, precisely because everything that was happening to us felt, while special and totally unique, completely incongruous with what I thought being J's person would be.

Meanwhile, J was on her own journey, somewhere I could not follow, at the edges of her body, which seemed to be going terrifyingly haywire. After the transplant and initial recovery, there was so much she once was able to do but no longer could. The losses she had to grieve accumulated and stretched before her. As she struggled with impairments and new chronic conditions she would have to live with, she became profoundly depressed. J spiraled into feelings of worthlessness, questioning what she could be to me now given her illness. "Why would you stay with me?" she asked. "I've been hoping my whole life for a girl like you," I would say. "And I'm certainly not going to let you go now."

Still, as her dependency on me increased, she struggled to feel desirable. In her mind, needing care was incompatible with being a valid lover and partner. I could not ease the pain of her losses, nor could I quell her insecurities, no matter how much I labored over her care. In fact, it seemed the more caregiving I did, the less lovable she felt. Such is the dehumanizing logic of ableism. Ableism deems some bodies inherently worth more than others—with your worth often hinging on your capacity to be independent and productive for the economy—such that being disabled or needing care become things to disdain in ourselves or in one another. It was almost as though J believed that needing real material care disqualified her from deserving the ideal of romantic love. So instead of being partners who felt we could meet each other's every need, we both ended up feeling we were not enough.

In the darkest moments, J and I would still cling to our romantic fantasy to get us through. We would revisit our early love letters to each other, and I continued to write more, attempting to generate more of our own mythology to sustain us: *You're the best love of my life I could have chosen. I chose you, still choose you, and don't you forget it.* When she was homebound or hospitalized for extensive periods while I was alone in the outside world, I would write in a journal, addressing every entry to her, telling her about the meal I was having or the interesting person I saw on the street. One of my entries was of me remembering that night at the bar when she first kissed me, this memory a trinket I would pull out for us whenever our faith in our capacity to carry on wavered.

As all this unfolded, I was a doctoral student in sociology, focusing on health and illness. I studied things like how people experience healthcare encounters, how people bring meaning and community to their illness or disability, and how our health and care systems work and where they don't. Each week, I also stood in front of a classroom and taught undergraduates about the politics of disability, including the idea that it's not bodies that need fixing, but an inaccessible and inhospitable society that does.

This is to say that when I met J, disability was already both an intellectual and political idea for me. But privately, I was devastated by the realities of J's impairments. They were always in flux, worsening, then improving, and sometimes multiple systems deteriorated at once. It was terrifying, I was struggling, and I felt like a hypocrite.

One afternoon, a fellow graduate student said to me after a seminar, "I couldn't do it. I don't know why you chose this, especially so early on in the relationship." We were perusing the drinks in the coolers of a bodega a few blocks from J's apartment. I winced, glad as I stared into the rows and rows of bottles ahead of me that we were in a situation that didn't require eye contact.

My classmate's words cut to the truth: that our society tends to believe it is acceptable to walk away from disabled people. That I should find a "better" partner, someone who didn't need so much care, someone more able-bodied. It stung too that this was said with such casualness. The assumed undesirability of disabled people is a sentiment that's status quo, ubiquitous and somehow acceptable. It was no wonder that J was internalizing these messages too. My classmate's words were a distillation of society and its ableist culture: When it came to the realities of illness and disability, everyone was poised to look away. And in abandoning someone like J, society was abandoning me too.

I don't know why you chose this. But none of it had felt like a choice, not really. Yes, J and I had chosen each other, and when she got sick, I stepped up to do whatever care needed doing. Somebody had to do it. And as her intimate partner, I was often the one. I felt responsible for keeping J alive.

Outside of a few of J's close friends, I didn't know where to turn. From friends to colleagues to people in my disability communities, I got the sense that the realities of my daily challenges as a caregiver were things I was supposed to push down, not talk about, keep private. My classmate's comment made it even clearer that it was J and me against the world.

———

About three years into my time as J's caregiver, I found myself searching the internet in the middle of the night for *caregiving* + *partner* or + *spouse*. The results returned something called the Well Spouse Association. I had never heard of it. In my years as a caregiver, no one had ever mentioned it to me. Once, early on in J's treatment, an oncology nurse asked me how I was. "It's understood that you matter too," she said. "Right?" I smiled and gave her the thumbs-up sign in response, but she didn't even see it. She hadn't slowed her pace as she walked by and had already disappeared behind a door.

I clicked through the Well Spouse Association website and learned they ran support groups in various cities—and there just happened to be one in Manhattan every month. The night I attended my first WSA meeting, I walked into a synagogue on the Upper West Side and followed signs taped up in a stairwell guiding me to a room. Inside, I found a dozen other people sitting in a circle.

Seated across the circle from me that evening was Ian, with whom I am still friends, nearly two decades later. He was in his sixties at the time, wearing a wrinkled blue button-up shirt, his hair mussed, bags under his eyes.

"Six weeks ago, my partner had a stroke," he explained, his expression blank. He seemed stunned, disoriented. She was seventy-four and had been on her way to go out dancing when she suddenly threw up in the back of a cab and lost consciousness. In the ER, he'd watched as she was rushed away on a gurney to have emergency surgery. Now, he was exhausted from caring for her twenty-four hours a day with no rest, from the hundreds of details he had to sort through and calls he had to answer, from the sudden swirl of medications, personal care needs, and insurance processes. Like me, this was his first WSA meeting.

Among the others present that night were those who had been caregivers for years, sometimes decades. They each shared their stories, and I was amazed at how much I could relate. One man's wife had a traumatic brain injury. One woman's husband had Parkinson's, and another woman's wife had various illnesses that rendered her homebound and needing care round the clock. There was someone in the group near my age. He was the only other person there with dark brown hair, a stark contrast to everyone else, who were older and gray. What I remember of him is that his wife had a terminal illness, and he was trying to process that the end was coming, although no one could quite tell him when, rendering every day a purgatory. The older members of the group shook their heads at him and me, saying we shouldn't have to know these things so young.

It was a strange club to join. But for the first time, I was surrounded by other people who knew intimately what I was going through. I had become so practiced at keeping the details of J's illness and all the complex feelings I had about it private. Until now, I had believed that what J and I were experiencing was extraordinary, the same way I believed that our love was extraordinary and had the power to conquer all. Now, looking around at the others, I was starting to realize how ordinary, how common my situation was, how normal. Illness and disability affect us all, because each of us inhabit a body that is fundamentally fallible. To be human is to try to exist within our bodies, and their catastrophes too. To love, then, is to provide care for those bodies. But this care cannot be feasibly provided by one person, and this comes into direct conflict with our expectations of romantic partners in particular.

Instead of knowing that what I was facing was as routine and human as it could be, I had spent years wearing my armor, trying to do it all alone. "That group saved my life," Ian told me later, reflecting on that first night of the group. I think it may have saved mine too.

I have no memory of what I said when it was my turn to introduce myself, but I imagine that I broke down, that I confessed I no longer felt like a functional human being, that I felt hopeless in the face of seemingly insurmountable demands, and alone in the responsibility of meeting them. But as the faces around me that night proved, I was definitely not alone.

———

Instead of happily ever after, falling in love with J had called upon me to increasingly fill a role that required meeting nearly every one of her needs. This was more than just providing emotional support when the person you love is suffering. This was the taking on of personal care work and professional levels of administrative and medical tasks, patient advocacy and coordination across different clinical departments in a hospital, as well as navigating the dizzying complexity of this country's social services and for-profit healthcare system. Looking back now, I realize that I wasn't just the one; I had become The One.

The One is tasked with the very real, ongoing, and unpaid work of caring for loved ones who are ill or disabled. In almost every family, someone is The One. These caregivers are bedside at the hospital, on the other end of the phone when a loved one is in crisis. They make the appointments, manage medications, and track symptoms. They are the person on the floor with their loved one when they cannot get up, the person who gives up sleeping through the night, who struggles against their guilt when they can't be there. They are knowledgeable about the intimacies and intricacies of their loved one's preferences and coordinate the thousands of tasks that need doing.

Data show that The One is usually, but not always, a woman. It may be the daughter raised and socialized to care—the person we think of as someone who naturally likes to do that work and seems to somehow have a knack for it, but in actuality was taught that they should. Maybe it's the youngest child, who is emotionally closest to a parent, or the oldest, who was always given more responsibility. Maybe the role is simply delegated to the person we think of as having the most caring heart.

Each of us is either already The One or know someone who has or will step into the role. That's because disability and illness are the most average things that can happen to us. Six in ten U.S. adults have a chronic condition, four in ten have more than one, and nearly 29 percent of the adult population is categorized as disabled. Not to mention that everyone struggles with short-term conditions, and if we live long enough we will age into disability at some point or another. Disability is not exceptional; it is utterly ordinary, everyday, all around us, in various shapes and forms.

Despite the fact that disabled people make up the largest minority group in the United States, we don't usually connect how America's care crisis directly relates to the abandonment of and hostility toward disabled people. In the latter half of the twentieth century, the disability rights movement rose up and advocated for, among other things, deinstitutionalization—that is, an end to the practice of automatically institutionalizing disabled people. In many ways, the movement won this fight, and we rightfully began to shift the site of care to people's homes and communities. But we did not also devise a robust public system to support families providing that care at home.

Now, with an estimated fifty-three million family caregivers in the United States—that's fifty-three million people who are The One—the sheer magnitude of the caregiving crisis stuns. We've chosen to abandon disabled people and caregivers by having minimal government programs for long-term care. Instead, we let our profit-driven healthcare system benefit from the millions of family caregivers who step up to bear the weight for free.

Few families can afford to pay out of pocket for even just a little help with home care. Family caregivers end up providing roughly 80 percent of the ongoing care their loved one needs, spending an average of about twenty-four hours per week providing care, even while a majority are employed in addition to their caregiving duties. There are so many family caregivers in the United States that if they were paid, their labor would be worth more than the amount spent on all other forms of professional long-term care combined. This includes nursing homes, private long-term care insurance, Medicaid-funded home and community-based services, Veterans Affairs services, and so on.

For ill or disabled people who are coupled, the work of care largely falls to their spouse or partner. Spousal caregiving is a unique place to dive into the politics of disability and care work because it is an encapsulation of our expectations around love, romance, sex, intimacy, and self-worth, as well as the social and legal contract of marriage and the duties of family. There's also something particularly isolating about caring for a spouse in a world that holds up our romantic relationship partner as the one meant to give us "everything." Looking back, I see now that myths about the power of romance have essentially hidden all the care that needs doing into the private sphere, cleverly smuggling it out of public view and into a "family matter," instead of a shared responsibility to one another. This arrangement is not sustainable. Those who are The One are not a bottomless resource, and disabled people deserve far better than to have their only path for receiving care consolidated in one person.

Even though my experience of becoming a caregiver was singular, in so many ways it was also plural. When I set out to write this book, I knew that I would have to tell my story, but I also knew that the focus could not be on my experience alone. So I interviewed forty-four caregivers across twenty-two states, from New England to Hawaii, whose partners had a wide variety of impairments from stroke to dementia to multiple sclerosis and more. To find spousal caregivers, I turned to the WSA leadership, and they circulated my information to support groups across the country. Many people were also in other online disease-specific groups, such that information about my research traveled far and wide.

The stories in this book give insight into how people come into the role of The One, how that experience unfolds, and what becoming The One does to us. And because the experiences of people on either side of caregiving are so inextricably linked, these stories equally include the perspectives of disabled and ill partners. This balance is intentional. If we don't see disability as a complex and deeply social experience *and* talk directly to disabled people about their experiences—including how they experience needing and receiving care—we are contributing to the erasure of disabled people from public life.

Having been a caregiver, I found that caregivers rarely get an opportunity to talk to one another, much less for our stories to be understood as part of a larger, shared phenomenon. And having spent time in both disability and caregiving communities, I've found that these two groups don't usually get to talk to each other either. In my caregiver support groups, we bemoaned the lack of programs or supports and how impossible it was to afford home care. But there was not a deeper discussion about *why* this was happening. With my disabled friends, we railed against the idea that our society doesn't plan for disability and doesn't include disabled people. But we didn't talk about the intensity of caregiving as an issue. Fostering such cross-community discussions is a crucial aim of *In Sickness and in Health*.

At the heart of this book is my belief that we must talk openly about the private pain we carry when it comes to caregiving, whether we are giving care, receiving care, or both. We are all coping with impossible demands, with grief and loss, and with the loneliness of being discarded by a culture that devalues caregiving because it devalues the people who need it. Staying silent only furthers our alienation, because it completes the cycle of state and societal abandonment in the cruelest of ways: It makes us think that we must face our most human experiences alone. But we are not alone. If you are The One, you are one of millions. If you are disabled or chronically ill, you are also one of millions. If anything is to change, we must listen to one another's stories, learn how to better love ourselves and each other, and build a different future of more collective care.

PART I

Without
a Net

———

The safety net is not a net!
It's a big fucking hole.
—Alice Wong 王美華, *My ICU Summer*

CHAPTER I

The Choice

BEFORE THE SUN WAS UP ON NOVEMBER 12, 2018, ÁNGEL woke up and put on his painter's whites and a white T-shirt with the Sherwin-Williams logo, just like he did every morning before work. He looked in the mirror, smoothed his graying hair, and adjusted his glasses. Then he pulled on his well-worn sneakers covered with paint splatter and made his way to the kitchen for coffee.

Ángel, a fifty-nine-year-old Puerto Rican man, worked as a house painter for a company that handled the contract work for a large retirement community near his central Florida home. He was part of the daily crew of people who took care of the warranty work on the homes.

"Part of the contract is that the homeowners get a year to nitpick the house," he told me, "and anytime they would see something, they'd call and they'd get someone to come out. If a fly poops on the wall, they call you and you have to paint it, and that does happen."

As she had been doing for nearly forty years, his wife and high school sweetheart, Kim, handed him his favorite breakfast: cherry Pop-Tarts. She also packed his food for the day, making sure he had plenty of water, Gatorade, and a soda to go with the ham sandwich, chips, and oatmeal cookies she placed inside his lunch box. After his coffee, Ángel grabbed his lunch, picked up his water jug, and kissed Kim before going out the front door.

He made his way across the porch, where their American flag flew, and into his red 1999 Ford Ranger with a silver diamond-plated toolbox and a gray ladder affixed to the back. As he climbed in and looked out the windshield, he noticed for the millionth time the two carriage lights that hung on either side of the garage.

"They'd been there for so dang long that the finish was worn off." If he could have just talked the landlord into letting him repaint them, it would have made a big difference to the look of the house. But no. He backed up and headed to work, traveling miles of roads lined by deep woods full of tall trees. He ate his Pop-Tarts while he drove.

As usual, he arrived at the worksite at seven. He and the other contractors, about half of whom were Latino men like Ángel and the other half white, stood around and chatted for a bit. There were about ten of them, ranging from nineteen years old to their sixties. They chatted about work or pondered where the planes flying overhead were going. Fiji, maybe? Somewhere warm and beautiful, they guessed.

His first appointment that day was with the homeowners of Rockhaven 32. He felt dread. "They were very difficult people, the kind of people who were always working the angle, always looking for something for free. And they were always looking to put the blame on you for something that is not entirely your fault." The issue he'd been called to take care of that day was very small: They didn't like the caulking around the windows on the inside. So Ángel spent his morning recaulking them.

Afterward, the homeowner complained to him that the caulk was still too wide. He explained to her that he couldn't possibly make it any thinner. "I can't do it any smaller or I'd have to put a pencil sharpener on my finger, and that'll make one hell of a bloody mess," he said.

Immediately, he regretted it. He couldn't believe he'd said that to her. It was completely out of character. He knew he couldn't speak to homeowners like that. He thought, *Why the hell did I say that? I know I'm going to get in trouble.*

Later that morning, he felt so exhausted that he called Kim. It was unusual for her to get a call from him during the day. *That's odd*, she thought. He called her again after lunch. Now things were getting downright strange. He told her yet again that he was tired and "felt out of sorts."

At the end of the workday, he left through the back gate. Driving home, he drifted a little to the right, but he hardly registered it. He pulled back into his lane and continued home to park, once again, between the two worn carriage lights. He sat there finishing his paperwork, documenting his mileage, and checking his job log.

Kim was on the sofa in the living room. He was a little late, but she knew he usually sat in the car for a few minutes to finalize everything for the day. He was either filling out paperwork, she thought, or finally eating his lunch so she wouldn't know he'd skipped it. She got up to meet him at the door, as she did every evening.

Just then, Ángel came through the front door and greeted Kim.

"Hi. What's up?" he said.

In his mind, he was just making normal conversation. But Kim had a terrified look on her face. Through the window, she had seen him walking and he was leaning to one side. Then, when he looked up to smile hello, one side of his mouth did not curl up like the other. The whole left side of his face was drooping.

Her stomach hit the floor. In a tone that Ángel had never heard from her before, she said, "You need to go to the doctor. Now."

Ángel was hesitant and tired. He just wanted to rest. He didn't know why Kim was so alarmed.

"You're listing, you're walking—you're listing to the left. It looks like you're drunk and you're going to fall down," she stammered.

"Okay," he relented. "But first I need a shower." His mother had always told him you can't go to the hospital without showering first. So he did. And there was nothing Kim could do about it.

She waited outside the bathroom, straining to hear, listening for every sound he made, ready to run in if he fell, her mind humming.

Moments later, Kim and Ángel sped to a nearby urgent care just a few miles down the road. As they got out of the car, a staff member ran out of the building.

"You need to get to the emergency room—now. We can call you an ambulance," the staff member said.

"No," Kim said, "I can do it faster."

The ER was forty minutes away, but she did it in twenty. As soon as they arrived, the nurses took his blood pressure. They took it two times. Three times. Another machine. Two more times, a third again. They thought the machine was broken. But over and over, his blood pressure read between 230 and 290 over approximately 145. Safe blood pressure should be more like 110 over 70.

They finally acquiesced: "It's not the machine. It's you."

The nurses started an IV and asked him questions about his medical background. But he had nothing to tell them. He had not seen a doctor since he was in the navy, and he had been discharged in 1983.

"You people don't understand what you charge," he said. "I can't afford it."

———

The lack of universal healthcare in the United States is the first gaping hole in the social safety net, and sure enough, people fall through. Ángel ended up in the hospital that day because he had gone into what's called a hypertensive crisis (when your blood pressure suddenly and drastically increases), which led to a massive stroke. It could have been prevented if he'd just had access to healthcare. Routine checkups would have spotted his high blood pressure and treated it earlier, most likely with a simple and widely available medication.

Although Ángel had been in the navy as a young man, he had never had access to healthcare through Veterans Affairs. After five years of active duty and one year in the reserves, he had an exit physical as part of the process of separating from service. He remembers the doctor telling him that if he didn't have a condition to claim as needing care for now, he couldn't add one later. He was healthy then and was never told about or offered healthcare through the VA again.

After the stroke in 2018, Kim reached out to the VA to ask if he could get healthcare through them. For months, she called. A couple of people told her they'd try to help, but they kept getting no for an answer, citing that it was because Ángel had served during peacetime. After months of getting nowhere, she gave up. Even their extended family members were shocked. Kim told me it didn't make sense. "You'd expect that you served your country, so you should get this." But as Ángel put it, "I'm disabled and a veteran, but I'm not a disabled veteran. The fine print." Another hole.

Ángel and Kim had been keen to sign up when the Affordable Care Act (ACA) was signed into law in 2010. But even though this program was meant to address the gaps in the American healthcare system, they could not afford the insurance premiums. By 2012, however, they realized they could finally afford it—but only for one person. As they sat at their kitchen table going over the numbers, they realized they were going to have to make the impossible choice of picking which one of them would get insurance.

On one hand, Kim had experienced recurrent and terrible migraines for years, and she knew she had a hernia that needed surgical treatment. On the other hand, Ángel felt fine, though when they went to the blood pressure kiosk in the pharmacy section of the grocery store, the numbers were often not good. Every time he sat in the plastic seat and slid his arm into the tube, the digital readout indicated his blood pressure was high.

They decided it should be Kim. She was fifty-one years old at the time and didn't know how much longer she could put off care for the serious issues she had. Their plan was that Kim would get taken care of first and then Ángel would follow, as soon as they could afford to add a second person to the policy. They would keep saving up.

In the years leading up to all this, Kim had also worked, but only part time, so her employer didn't offer her health insurance. Their calculus would have been different if she had been able to get insurance through her job, but federal law does not require employers to provide healthcare coverage for part-time workers. And about four years before she rushed Ángel to the hospital, she'd had to quit her job entirely to become a full-time caregiver to her elderly father who had moved in with them because there were no other options.

The loss of Kim's income while caring for her father meant the couple was even further from affording health insurance during that time. It's not uncommon for women to have to leave the workforce in order to become The One. As sociologist Jessica Calarco writes in *Holding It Together*, millions of women in the United States have no other choice but to stop working to become the care system for children and other family members. In this case, Kim became The One for her father. As he grew increasingly frail, they had no other choice but to rely on Kim to care for him full time until he died on the floor in the couple's home just a few months before Ángel's stroke. As Calarco has said, "Other countries have social safety nets; the U.S. has women."

Healthcare was first linked to employment after the Stabilization Act of 1942. Prior to that, medical insurance was not part of the state's domain; medicine didn't have nearly as much to offer as it does now in terms of treatments and interventions, so whatever insurance existed was privately bought and uncommon. As World War II broke out, however, there were too few workers in the United States; economists, worried about inflation, warned employers that raising pay to attract workers could tank the economy. As a result, businesses decided to compete for workers by entering a benefits arms race. Health insurance thus began to be offered as a work benefit in the context of war, itself another common pathway to disability.

A year after linking insurance to employers, the IRS made employer-based health insurance tax-free. This move cemented the linkage of healthcare insurance and employment. If group health insurance plans were tax exempt, then it was cheaper than individual private insurance. But because different employee statuses are built into U.S. labor law, employers can take advantage of various statuses to avoid offering healthcare coverage to their workers and taking on these costs when they can.

Part-time workers, as we've seen, are excluded from coverage; so are workers in the individual contractor category. Ángel never missed a day of work, putting in a full day every week Monday through Friday. But as was standard in the construction industry, he was considered self-employed. So, while U.S. healthcare costs have skyrocketed because it is a for-profit industry, employers can also get away with not covering workers like Ángel, who worked the equivalent of full-time hours too. They do this by categorizing employees as independent contractors, which is what Ángel was as a house painter at the retirement community. Independent contractors are considered self-employed and therefore responsible for their own healthcare, retirement, and so on.

There just aren't other feasible options for getting care without insurance. In the United States as of 2024, the average cost of a physical exam with a primary-care doctor without insurance was $397. And that's just walking through the door. This is already prohibitive for millions of people, including Kim and Ángel. And the Federal Reserve reports that 37 percent of Americans don't have enough money to pay for a $400 emergency.

The $397 cost to see a doctor doesn't include the cost of medications that might be prescribed, which can be astronomical for ongoing chronic conditions. Nor does it pay for any follow-up appointments, testing, labs, or other investigatory procedures that may need to occur before treatment can commence and be maintained.

After scrimping and saving, however, the couple's budget finally allowed for Ángel to be added to the ACA policy in the fall of 2018. They signed him up and waited for coverage to begin. His plan was to see a doctor right after Thanksgiving. His first primary-care appointment was just two weeks away as he headed out to the shift where he would caulk the windows at Rockhaven 32.

CHAPTER 2

Fade to Black

DESPITE HIS BLOOD PRESSURE BEING DANGEROUSLY HIGH IN the ER, Ángel still didn't really feel much of anything besides tired. Scans and X-rays were ordered, so he slid himself onto a gurney headed down to radiology. When he got there, the radiologist and nurse asked him to transfer onto the hard, metal bed of the CAT scan machine. This was when Ángel realized he was in trouble.

"I couldn't sit up. I couldn't stand up. I couldn't move my left side at all. It took two orderlies and a nurse to move me."

Prior to that, he had been able to feel his left side and move it. But on the trip to radiology, something had broken within him. He gritted his teeth through it. He didn't want to complain. After the imaging was done, they admitted him as a stroke patient. He was hooked up to monitors and given medication to bring his blood pressure down. That's when the pain started.

In the middle of his upper left arm, just below the shoulder, he felt a strange and deeply painful sensation. There was pain below his hip too. "It was as if my arm and leg had been cut off with a sword, a clean cut straight across, all the way through." The muscles and nerves at each end of his body were on fire. The pain radiated down his left side, and his left hand became a club, his fingers contracting to the point where he thought his fingernails would go clear through his palm. The toes on his left foot curled under. "It hurt like you wouldn't believe."

"And then," he told me, "things went bad."

He hadn't been scared before this. He hadn't been scared as they drove to the ER, he had just felt hesitation and dread. He hadn't even been scared when his blood pressure was so high. Reading the reactions of other people, the look on Kim's face and her tone of voice, he had a feeling that none of this was going to be good. But it wasn't until this moment that he actually felt deep fear.

"They had me all hooked up with wires. I'm lying in the bed, and I'm looking up, and there's a big school clock on the wall, and there's some posters on the right. I start losing vision, and everything starts to slowly turn white and disappear. I had socks on. Hanes. They say Hanes on the toe, and all of a sudden, my feet disappear, I can't see anything."

The medication meant to bring his blood pressure down had stopped his heart.

Kim does not like to talk about this. We slowly broached the topic together as I sat with her in the couple's living room in October 2021. Ángel was in the kitchen cleaning up, so we had some privacy. We had talked multiple times before this visit, over video and telephone, and I shared that I had been a caregiver too, that I had some sense of her pain. So now we took a deep breath together and dug as far into the memory of that day as Kim could go.

She had been sitting on Ángel's right side, holding his hand, when the machines coded and beeped, when his eyes rolled back, when she saw him leave. She was the one right there next to him before the staff rushed in. And what more could she say about it? What is there to say when you're watching this happen to your partner of nearly forty years?

Ángel was born in Puerto Rico, but his family moved to the mainland a few months later. They settled near Washington, D.C., because his father worked for the federal government. Shortly after, his parents separated. It turned out that his father had a secret second family with children around the same ages as Ángel and his siblings. His father moved in with that family instead.

There was very little left over for Ángel's family. On payday, his father showed up for a few minutes and gave his mother $120 for three kids, "to pay the bills, water, electric, telephone, trash, heat, and groceries, and whatever we needed for school." They didn't officially get divorced until Ángel was twenty years old, but the ritual of bringing over a small amount of money continued until then.

Throughout his childhood, his mother worked odd jobs, including at a factory, and made very little. Ángel and his siblings survived on rice and beans. They made them every single day. "You grab mom's pot. You fill the water to the waterline, the stain mark, then you take the cup and dump it in. That's what you do."

Ángel still isn't much of a cook. "I'm terrible because I use a pair of pliers and a soup can." It was Kim who showed him life. In high school, he started going to her house for meals. "I had no idea that there was more than one fork or more than one butter knife. But I went to her family's house for dinner, and they had salad forks and dinner forks. Then they had cocktail forks and dessert forks and this fork and that fork."

He was rough around the edges then, with odd ways of "cooking" on his own. "I kept a pair of channel locks in the kitchen and a spoon. I'd open a can of something, warm it up on the stove, eat with the spoon, wash it off, throw the can away, and put my channel locks back in the drawer." He wasn't on his own for long though. Ángel and Kim got married young and "he's been spoiled ever since," Kim giggled.

Kim also grew up in the suburbs of Washington, D.C. They met in high school when they were both in the Junior Reserve Officers' Training Corps or JROTC. Kim was a sophomore and Ángel a senior. He was squadron commander, and she volunteered for almost anything one could volunteer for. "And then I take over. The phrase is 'You've been Kimmed.'" She laughed. They butted heads over how to do things when they met, mostly on leadership points. They disagreed over how to get people motivated to follow. One night, they went as a pair to a dinner at another school. Their mutual friends pushed them to go together. It seemed they had all decided that Kim and Ángel had to stop their bickering and just get together. The night went swimmingly. "We got along. We've been together ever since," Kim said.

Ángel graduated in 1977. He tried to attend college for a brief period, a four-year state school nearby, but still lived at home. He lasted two semesters before dropping out. He was taking organic chemistry and astrophysics, but he found it hard to focus on school. He wanted to get as far away from his family as he could, and that meant enlisting in the navy. He went on a six-year tour to the Mediterranean, the Persian Gulf, and everywhere in between. He and Kim spoke on the phone and wrote letters. Back home, she attended a nearby community college. On a trip home in 1981, they got married.

Kim's parents were surprised. And some in her family, which was white, had a hard time with the fact that Ángel was Latino. "There were some tough times there for a while with family members."

Meanwhile, Ángel was overseas until the end of his six-year tour, in 1983. He decided not to reenlist and instead settled into married life with Kim. They stuck around D.C., and Ángel got a job managing a 1-hour photo shop in Dupont Circle.

"That was during the Iranian terrorist time, and he had the beard," Kim said, handing me a photo of the two of them sitting under the blossoming cherry trees at the Tidal Basin. In the picture, Ángel is tall, brown-skinned, with a full, thick, dark beard, looking at the camera. "You couldn't tell what he was besides scary," she said. Once, a man came into the photo shop and had a fit. He was banging on the counter, demanding to see management. In came Ángel, the manager. "He took one look at me and said, 'I'm fine. I'm fine. Goodbye.' He backed his way out of the store, and we never saw him again."

Years later, after moving to Georgia, Ángel wanted to start his own house-painting business while he worked as a contractor for others to make ends meet. "I couldn't be successful. I couldn't convince people that I could do the best job." He repeatedly lost bids. "They ask you to come and bid a job, and yet you find out they took another bid that is significantly lower or even higher. You can drive past the job site a few weeks later and see it is horrible work. They didn't want to pay me five dollars, but they'd pay that guy twenty dollars for that crap?" He just didn't get it. "What was it about me that turned them off?"

Sometimes when he showed up at a job site, it was to work as a contractor for the person who had won the bid. It was demoralizing, and he could tell by the money they paid him that the contractor was hired at a much higher price than what Ángel bid. "There was something about my personality, my mannerisms, my something, that made them feel cautious, wary. It made them feel so uncomfortable that they went somewhere else." It was small-town, rural Georgia, he told me. "If we don't know your mama, your preacher, you just don't fit in."

And so, his plan to own his own house-painting business never took off. "I've had some successful jobs, yes, but overall, the business failed." He kept on working as a contractor. Their son grew up.

They moved to Florida in 2015. Ángel liked the steady contract work he got at the retirement community, even if he didn't like all the residents he worked for. The years unfurled, until that moment in the hospital, amid the chaos and the beeping and the frantic pace of them working on Ángel, when Kim thought, *Please, don't do this to me.*

"It was hard to watch him being resuscitated. It was hard to sit there and watch him go so still, and his eyes roll back and know where he went," Kim told me.

He was dangerously close to not being able to hold on. But he came back. He saw the wall clock once again. He saw his feet, Hanes across the toe. Then he became aware of Kim, sitting by his side just like she had been for nearly forty years, holding his hand.

———

Ángel had a stroke because he didn't have access to routine, preventative healthcare to manage his blood pressure. He didn't have access to that care because we yoke healthcare to certain kinds of jobs, using one's working status as a measure for deserving care, rather than viewing care as a universal human need. This approach leads to more people experiencing more catastrophic health conditions and disabilities later.

Ironically, ableism—our valuing of some bodies over others

for their productivity and independence—helps to explain why we don't have universal healthcare or a robust care infrastructure. It is ironic because ableism, which is also characterized by the devaluation and denigration of disability, tells us that only certain people are valuable and therefore worthy of care. But the consequence of not having universal access to care is, in fact, more disability.

One pivotal point for understanding the entrenchment of ableism in our care-related policies occurred at the turn of the twentieth century, when U.S. progressives launched a massive national campaign centered around the emergent ideology of eugenics. Eugenics is a set of explanations that blames broader social problems on some individuals' bad genes. The idea is that social problems occur not because of bad policies or unequal systems, but because of *who some people innately are.* It is a seductive explanation for social problems and for the complexities of the world, but it is wrong.

Fundamentally, it is an ideology based on the twin pillars of white supremacy and ableism; central to eugenics is the intertwined pursuit of both a racially "pure" nation made up of those deemed superior through their whiteness *and* a curated population of those whose bodies and minds adhere to ideals around independence and productivity. For example, public campaigns of the time explicitly asked white women to birth more babies to save the country from rising rates of immigration and also provided information on how to identify who was an "idiot" or an "imbecile" or "feeble-minded," so that they could be institutionalized and even sterilized.

Most people tend to think of eugenics as a set of concrete past actions occurring in some kind of discrete historical moment, but a century later its ideas are still embedded in our care policies (and beyond—in the lead-up to the 2024 election,

Donald Trump made claims about immigrants and their "bad genes"). Such eugenic beliefs that there are "bad genes" and resultantly "dependent people" show how intertwined ableism and racism are and how present it still is. Indeed, in 2018, the year Ángel had his stroke, a HuffPost/YouGov poll found that Americans still significantly overestimate the number of Black people who benefit from federal programs. That is, the idea of welfare is racialized and drenched in connotations of deservingness, rife with assumptions that certain people—namely disabled people and people of color—are a burden, rather than admitting we are all humans with bodies that need care.

As a result, the federal welfare programs we do have tend to take a reluctant, piecemeal approach to providing care for people who employer-based insurance leaves out. The largest of these programs are Medicaid (which covers low-income adults and children) and Medicare (which mostly covers those over sixty-five). President Lyndon B. Johnson signed Medicare and Medicaid into law in 1965, and while people may assume otherwise, white people are the majority of Medicaid beneficiaries.

Then there was the ACA, which Kim and Ángel had pinned their hopes on. Even the fights over this policy, occurring during Obama's first term, echoed eugenic narratives. As Jonathan Metzl documents in *Dying of Whiteness*, he spoke with many white people who often did not support the ACA since it would broadly expand government support in the realm of healthcare, which would include providing nonwhite people access to care. They seemed to prefer the denial of universal care (and thus not having healthcare themselves and undermining their own health) than extending access to care to those they deemed undeserving of it. (It is also worth noting the political power that disabled people have begun to amass; later in 2017, it was disability activists who protested to save the ACA when it was threatened with being overturned.)

While the ACA did expand access to healthcare, it did not create universal care. Rather, it built on the system we already have and it sold healthcare as a commodity. Ángel and Kim, like so many others, still couldn't afford it. Healthcare costs continue to skyrocket, and the gig economy booms. Even if people are ostensibly "productive"—meaning that they are workers who produce capital—it seems that having a job may still not be enough to qualify you as "deserving" of care. In fact, fewer and fewer are eligible for healthcare as workers are increasingly categorized as independent contractors. And Black and Latine Americans, like Ángel, are more likely to be working in the gig economy than other demographic groups.

———

After the stroke, after the fade to black and the return to the living, Ángel was sent to that intervening space between hospital and home: rehab. He was paralyzed on his entire left side and struggled with vision changes, like going blind in his left eye, and other surprises he slowly discovered about his body. His six-week rehab stint was, overall, an isolating and devastating experience. While in rehab, he was forced to confront the new landscape of his limitations alone.

Ángel had always been stressed out, "a double-A, triple-A personality, always trying to be in control," as he described it. He held tightly to the idea of being able to control his body now, to make it beat the stroke. "I'll recover in thirty days, babe. We'll be out of here. It will be behind us," he told Kim at the time.

"Dumbass," he muttered to himself as he and I sat in his

living room while he recounted this story. Here he was, three years later, still wheeling around his house in his wheelchair and using his "good leg" to get us coffee while Kim was at work. Then he said soberly, "I wanted that, but it was totally unrealistic."

As the weeks in rehab wore on, it all started to hit him. "I can't stand without help; I can't walk without help. They ask me to get on all fours and I can't. I can't do the bicycle. I can't do the arm bicycle. It was a hard pill to swallow." He'd taken being able to do those things for granted for so long, for his whole nearly sixty-year life, that he struggled to come to terms with relearning how to stand up, or even just to stay vertical.

Lying in bed at night, he'd contemplate it all. Kim wasn't allowed to stay with him overnight, and her absence was hard on him. Night was when the darkness came.

"The anxiety and the stress and the fear, all I saw was an ocean of blackness. What comes to mind is that that's the color of time. Time is black." Each night, Ángel grew more and more terrified. He feared "being lost, being adrift in that ocean of blackness forever."

When these thoughts came, Ángel couldn't feel Kim's heartbeat next to his, reaffirming his own. He couldn't reach for her. He couldn't be comforted. This threw Ángel over the edge; being asked to process what had happened to him in the middle of all this loss and confusion, indeed at times disorientation, was already too much. And then not to have his wife with him, his love, his lifeline? There was no other support. Of course he was reliant entirely on Kim to get through this. She was The One.

CHAPTER 3

Discharged

KIM STAYED AS MANY HOURS EACH DAY AS THE REHAB would let her. Then she went home and spent hours on the phone with family members reliving the day, telling them what had transpired the day of the stroke and where Ángel was at now. It felt like running a comms department, trying to figure out who needed to know what and to answer all their questions.

After the calls, she sat with her worries. Would she be able to take care of him? He would eventually come home, and she was keenly aware that once he did, she would be responsible for it all, yet she didn't know what the scope of that responsibility would be.

In turning it over in her mind, she got busy where she could. It felt better to *do something*. She measured the doorways to make sure they were wide enough for a wheelchair, which luckily they were. She made sure he'd be able to wheel into the bathroom, and that the bed in the bedroom was set up so he could get into it as well.

Still, the questions and the worries flooded her thoughts. Would his diet change? Would someone come and do physical therapy with him? Would he ever stop being disoriented about whether it was day or night? He had been calling her at

2:00 a.m. each day, saying good morning and telling her it's time to get up.

And then Kim suddenly realized, "He's not going to be working anymore. Now what?" His house-painting work had been their only source of income. How would they pay for the basics? There was no way she could go back to work, she needed to be home to take care of him. There were so many unanswered questions.

But of course Kim desperately wanted him home. She missed her husband. Sure, she was scared, but she was also sure that he would be happier and better off if they were together, and so would she. I spoke to so many other older adults across the country whose spouse had had a heart attack, a stroke, or an accident, and who had also followed the trajectory of being hospitalized and then sent to rehab. Many of them told me about their conviction that they would be The One to give the best, most attentive care to their partner—if they could just get them home.

Spouses were often desperate to take on the role at this early stage of acute need, still reeling and running on adrenaline. They were ready to jump in and help their newly disabled spouse vanquish their condition; overcome with what had happened, they were eager to regain some sense of "normal." Over time, of course, the realities would set in and their understanding—and energy levels—would change, but their loved one coming home was a milestone they all couldn't wait for.

As one man in New York City who was The One for his wife told me, spouses and other family members provide "exquisite" care, while sometimes facilities can provide anything but. I also spoke to a woman in Minnesota who was The One for her husband, who'd had a motorcycle accident that resulted in paralysis, broken limbs, and a series of strokes. She said she could not wait to get him home, especially when she found out that the night nurse would "put a urinal wrapped in a towel between his legs when she got on shift so he wouldn't bug her during the night."

Writing about nursing homes and other forms of institutional care, the journalist Sara Luterman explains these sites allow for an economy of scale. "Feeding, washing, and otherwise seeing to the needs of elderly and disabled residents all at once is more efficient than addressing those needs on an individual basis. But this efficiency comes at the expense of human dignity." A lack of regulations and standards, among other things, impact the quality of care that people may receive in facilities. Staff ratios are particularly important; research has routinely shown that lower staff-to-patient ratios result in better care and outcomes.

It is no wonder, then, that when polled most Americans don't want to be in a facility, especially a long-term facility, when they need care. They want to stay home, to "age in place." But without home-care infrastructure, it falls to The One to take on the roles of physical therapist, appointment scheduler, medication manager, and all-around assistant in addition to their usual domestic duties. What we don't talk about regarding aging in place is that without actual care infrastructure to support it, it requires someone to be The One to make it happen.

Kim put in her hours to train for this new and unexpected job. At the rehab, staff repeatedly modeled different techniques for her to move Ángel from lying to sitting, sitting to standing, on and off the toilet, into and out of the car, and so forth. This is called transferring. They kept doing it to prepare Kim for the handoff. The key, they said, was to transfer him in a safe way that kept him from falling, but also to make sure Kim knew how to do it without injuring her back.

"Watch what we do," the staff said. Kim watched. She studied them closely. They even had a little fake car to practice with. "They tried to show her how to keep me from falling out of the car trying to get me into it," Ángel told me. But it wasn't a real car, and it certainly didn't approximate their car, so it wasn't a particularly useful exercise.

Even though learning to transfer safely is deeply important and helpful, that was pretty much it in terms of what resources the couple were offered. The staff didn't seem to have anything more than that, nor the deeper knowledge of what it's like to become a disabled person. No one seemed to realize Ángel's new life would require far more than just learning to transfer. No one seemed to know about the worries Kim carried. She didn't know who to talk to because she didn't know what to anticipate and therefore didn't have the language yet to ask questions.

"The staff only knew what they learned in class," Kim mused, looking back on this. "They were babies, truly. Young, strong as oxen, and newly out of school." They did not seem to know what it meant to live as a disabled person or that disability communities exist. "I don't know if it was just the facility that he was in or if it's everywhere. I have a feeling it's everywhere."

Kim is right. A limited imagination of what disability means is everywhere. In the academic field of disability studies, scholars have been writing for decades that society in general has a flawed and narrow view of disability. People often see it as only an individual medical problem. This view of disability is known as the medical model, and it describes how we tend to see disability through a lens of deficiency or diagnosis, as an individual medical tragedy that overshadows everything else about a person and isn't understood as a social experience or political issue. If you take any Disability Studies 101 class, and I have taught many of them, the medical model is a common starting point.

As part of the medical model logic that pervades our culture, medical professionals, including rehab staff, are often seen as (and therefore educated to see themselves as) the sole authority over disabled people. If disability is only understood as a medical deficiency, then what else would there be to consider? With such a limited approach, it is easy to think that the only knowledge we need to have about a stroke patient is the specific physiological effects of the stroke. It's not that medical knowledge is unimportant—it is important to treat various impairments well—it's that the medical characteristics of an impairment are only a tiny part of a disabled person's story.

What Ángel needed most at this point was some practical advice on how to be a disabled person in the world, and even some emotional real talk on how to adjust, to know that there was life on the other side, to hear that a disabled life can be a good life. He might have benefited from being connected to other people like him who had been there already and had some wisdom to share. That's the problem with seeing disability only as an individual medical problem; it forecloses our ability to think of it as a deeply social phenomenon, as about identity, as about navigating a world that devalues your life as a disabled person every step of the way.

Ángel didn't get any of that perspective. No one talked to him about any of the challenges he'd face or how to cope with them, or told him that disability communities exist. Despite ostensibly being in a place where disabled people are gathered—a rehab—there was no discussion of what it means to become disabled, broadly speaking. The patients didn't talk to each other, and neither did family members. And so Ángel's mind kept on reeling. *How do I find my way? How do I cope with the losses, with looking down at this new body that I don't recognize, with the changes in my vision? What about sex? What about making something out of this new thing that I am?*

Kim didn't get any information either. "It would have been nice," Kim told me, "even if you got five spouses together and said, 'Okay, this is what you're going to have to deal with when you get home.'" Instead, all the care that needed doing was consolidated onto her. There wasn't even acknowledgment that there was no system in place for the care work; it was just assumed that *she* would be the system. It was a given that you go home and your spouse or other family member will be The One to care for you and that was it. Her mind further spun out.

"When you get to rehab, you're not taught what it would be like when you get home, it's like here you go, you're trusting me with this but now what do I do?" she said. As discharge approached and the anticipation ratcheted up, Kim braced herself for the transition. Until then, she hadn't been doing hands-on care for Ángel. Now it was time. She would be The One to take over and assist with the showering, toileting, transferring in and out of a chair, and getting in and out of bed. She would be responsible for all his activities of daily living (bathing, eating, dressing, toileting), known as ADLs. Neither Ángel nor Kim was sure what any of this meant for their future. And they didn't feel prepared.

At discharge, a day mixed with fear and excitement, Ángel was still unsteady, incontinent, and emotionally fragile. As she gathered his things and got him in the wheelchair, Kim realized she was not only going to have to do the basic day-to-day care, but she would need to take on the task of emotional and social support as well. But this too was thrust upon her without any resources.

Well, except for one of note.

As Ángel left the rehab, staff wished them luck and handed them a pamphlet. The topic? Suicide prevention. Apparently, it seemed the rehab staff assumed Ángel might prefer to be dead.

CHAPTER 4

Decertified

KIM WAS DAUNTED. *ÁNGEL IS TALL, SHE IS SHORT, AND SHE* would be doing heavy lifting all day every day transferring him. She helped with showering, toileting, getting in and out of a chair, and getting in and out of bed. She was petrified of him falling.

Ángel kept telling her not to be scared and to try to let the fear of him falling go. "Just do what you can and if I fall, I fall. That's part of it. Don't try and stop me, because all you're going to do is get hurt, and we need somebody who's not hurt to call for help." She tried not to psych herself out.

Just before Ángel came home from rehab, the staff visited and conducted a home check. "They spent an hour checking the house to make sure that, I guess, I didn't have knives out or whatever," Kim explained. They set up the shower chair in their bathroom on that visit, but it turns out that they set it up backward.

"They had him sliding in bad arm first. There was nothing for him to grip on to, to help slide himself in. And you put wet feet in a wet tub. . . ." She trailed off. Turns out, when it came time for Kim to assist Ángel with his first shower at home, there was a fall, a terrifying sliding down, and it scared her. She could not stop the visions of him hitting his head on the floor or breaking something. She was terrified he would be hurt on her watch. They did sponge baths for months after that because she was so scared. Eventually, someone suggested they turn the chair so that his "good side" goes in first, and this worked better.

But she was right to be scared. Just days after returning home, there was an incident. Ángel became deathly pale, disoriented, clammy, his heart rate skyrocketed, and he could barely move on his own at all. Kim and her brother, who happened to be visiting, thought he was having a second stroke and called 911.

The worst part wasn't seeing them take Ángel out on the stretcher, it was the interrogation after. "It was like an interrogation as to whether or not you did it to this person," Kim said. They grilled her, "What did you feed him? Did you give him his meds right?" She felt like they were trying to find fault with something she did.

"I understand that they're doing their job, getting the information, but you're already feeling overwhelmed and underqualified." She showed them his med list, she shook her head, she was just trying to do everything right, but whatever she did as The One, it never seemed to be enough.

It turned out that Ángel had a serious heart condition that they hadn't known about. He had a hole in his heart and needed a procedure to treat it. He got the care he needed for that, and yet again he came home. They were lucky. His ACA insurance policy had begun. That was how they were able to get him the emergency care, as well as the rehab, and even some physical therapy sessions at home after the stroke.

When he came home this time, they focused on picking up where they left off, centering Ángel's recovery as a full-time job for both him and Kim. He needed to retrain his synapses, practice movement, and build his strength. And he was desperate to do so. But the ACA covered only eighteen sessions of outpatient physical therapy for the year, and that wasn't nearly enough. He quickly used them up, and then they were forced to get creative.

Since Kim was unable to leave the house for a job since she was The One around the clock, she added new duties to her already expanding list. There was no other choice. They simply couldn't afford to pay out of pocket for real PT, and they were told he needed sessions three to four times a week. She consulted YouTube for PT exercises; that was her training. She built steps and platforms out of scrap wood to "train" on, following the videos and making do with what they had in their garage.

They were already practiced at jerry-rigging things. Not long after Ángel got home the first time, they realized they would need ramps. He wasn't going to be able to get into the house in the wheelchair without them. But ramps are expensive, and they couldn't afford to pay for them. So Kim's brother and their son built them from various scraps of plywood and random bits of wood in the garage. They weren't pretty, they didn't meet "standards," but they got the job done.

Despite all their efforts, Ángel just didn't regain as much mobility as he had wanted. Maybe it was because they didn't have the resources to get top-line and regular PT, but he kept trying. Four years afterward, Ángel felt like he hadn't accomplished as much as he had wanted. He wanted to get better not just for himself but so that Kim didn't have to work so hard caring for him all the time.

With Kim's duties as The One growing by the day, Ángel not being able to be left alone, and no source of income in sight, it was all coming down on them. They were not going to be able to live without an income of any kind. While Ángel was still in rehab, scared about how they were going to survive, they had turned to the state and started the process of applying to one of our few safety nets: Social Security Disability Insurance (SSDI).

————

SSDI is for those who are not of retirement age yet, but are too disabled to work. It is housed in the Social Security Administration, or SSA. This federal agency processes claims for disability, and with 8.7 million people receiving SSDI, it is the largest safety-net program for disabled Americans. But once again, it's tied to work. SSDI is based on your work history or "work credits" that you accrue through SSA deductions in your paycheck, alongside your disability status.

It's a common assumption that if you're disabled, then you simply get SSDI as a substitute for working and you are taken care of. But this is a myth; it's far more complicated than that. In 2022, the Center for American Progress found that the majority of SSDI beneficiaries (58 percent) were receiving less than the then-average $1,362 monthly benefit, and nearly a third (29 percent) were receiving less than $1,000. Monthly payments are calculated based on the disabled person's former work earnings. This means people receive wildly different levels of payments, with most receiving income that is not anywhere close to livable. By 2025, the average monthly SSDI benefit was only around $1,581.

SSDI does not provide ongoing care and support for disabled people. Rather, the process of becoming eligible for SSDI is only "a legal process of decertifying a body for work," write Artie Vierkant and Beatrice Adler-Bolton in *Health Communism: A Surplus Manifesto*. SSDI is only about making sure that "the benefit applicant is truly biologically incapable for work, through 'no fault of their own.'"

Elaborate methods of gatekeeping are also deployed because of a continued and entrenched belief that programs for disabled people are plagued with waste, fraud, and abuse. Most people have to go through a long determination process that is onerous and overwhelming. Medical symptoms must be documented in detail, and the diagnosis must be expected to last at least one year or result in death.

Kim and Ángel didn't have time to wait. They would be homeless without SSDI. In preparing his application, Kim told me that she "crossed every *t*, dotted every *i*, double-checked everything five times, and had a friend of mine look over everything to see if I missed anything." They were asked to come in for an evaluation, the next step in the process, just a couple of months after the application was turned in.

Kim and Ángel made their way to an SSA-approved facility to meet with an evaluator. Ángel was asked if he could stand and take one step forward. They both gritted their teeth. "They could deny it because he could walk and possibly work, all because he could stand and take one step," Kim explained. But Ángel could clearly not do this easily; the evaluator took one look at him and acquiesced that he was "actually disabled," and when it was over he said that he had to be careful with his evaluations since "people cheat the system."

I spoke to dozens of other people who described their experience applying for SSDI. For almost everyone else I spoke to, it was a long and complex process, requiring thick files and binders to be filled with every tiny piece of their medical and financial information that could be found. The process also involved additional requests from the SSA for clarification, or rejection due to small clerical errors in the paperwork. To be successful, in fact, it's best to hire a lawyer. The SSA denies about 66 percent of all cases. A study released in 2018 by the Government Accountability Office showed that people who hired lawyers or who had other representatives were nearly three times more likely to be approved.

Waiting for approval and being denied means starting all over again, waiting even longer, all while not being able to work and thus not having income. Data show that the length of time it takes to get approved for SSDI is getting markedly worse. In the late 2010s, the SSA typically processed applications within 110 to 120 days. This was around the time that Kim and Ángel went through the process. However, by the end of 2023, wait times for SSDI averaged 228 days, nearly eight months. These wait times don't just make disabled people more precarious and less safe for longer, they kill people. In the 2023 fiscal year, the SSA reported that thirty thousand people died while waiting for their SSDI determination, due to what the then Social Security commissioner called a "customer service crisis."

It's also not a one-time qualification, but something you have to requalify for even if your condition is permanent or degenerative. Such endless paperwork and ever-expanding administrative tasks are what legal scholar Elizabeth Emens calls "disability admin." This may look different depending on illness type and trajectory but, she writes, "this labor takes a serious toll" on disabled people and caregivers alike.

I can remember whole days and weeks lost to trying to get the right paperwork, learning how to use the right language, knowing who to give the forms to, and so on. While J had already qualified for and gotten Medicare and Medicaid before we met due to her previous bout with cancer, there were more and other state systems whose navigation felt similar to the experiences I'd heard about from others.

More than three years after her transplant, J was still struggling with chronic conditions and mobility restrictions that she acquired as a result of posttransplant complications. Her mobility was affected; she was unable to go up and down stairs, so we moved out of our walk-up apartment and into an apartment in my aunt's building because it had an elevator. She also could not use the subway, and she needed a cane for short distances and a wheelchair for longer distances. To make sure I could safely get her out of the apartment building and into our car for appointments in Manhattan from Brooklyn, we needed a handicapped parking permit. We also needed to get her signed up for Access-A-Ride, an NYC paratransit system that disabled New Yorkers must use because much of mass transit is not accessible to them.

I downloaded the Access-A-Ride forms, J filled out what she could, but her grip strength was deteriorating, so I finished them for her. Then we had to obtain doctor's letters and medical records. After the application was processed, she would have an in-person verification process, as Ángel and Kim had done at the SSA facility. This required driving deep into Brooklyn, way out on Coney Island Avenue near the ocean, to a nondescript building that has a mock-up of a city bus inside. Her appointment was made weeks in advance, and the only appointments available were in the middle of the day. And of course, you never know how long you'll have to wait or if the appointments run even remotely on time.

On the day of our appointment, I blocked off the whole day to take her, which meant I couldn't work, but by then I was used to taking multiple days a week off for taking care of such tasks. That morning, it took us a while to get out the apartment door, down the long hallway with her cane, onto the elevator, and out the front door to the car that I had to get and pull around from street parking. She had to stand, holding on to the wrought-iron fence in front of our building, while I ran down the block to the car. Having a handicap permit would have let us park the car in the same spot up front all the time, which was much safer.

At the facility, J was asked to demonstrate how she walked, to try to get up by herself, climb the bus stairs, and transfer in and out of the fake bus seats, and so on, while someone watched her for signs of "fraud." I assisted so she wouldn't fall. It was a humiliating and rage-inducing experience for both of us. We had pinned our hopes on receiving this benefit, but in submitting to a process that essentially asked for proof of J's right to exist, we were left feeling as though we had given a piece of ourselves away.

———

Our minimal social safety nets are often infused with a sense of suspicion about deservingness, which usually relates to how "real" one's disability is perceived to be. It is demoralizing and dehumanizing, and I think that's the point. The irony is that fraud is rare. The SSA reports the "fraud rate" is less than 1 percent when it comes to disability claims. Yet the belief that disability claims are frequently fraudulent persists in the public sphere and, as the comment of Ángel and Kim's evaluator shows, may even infiltrate the attitudes of agency staff.

In 2022, I wrote a short piece for *The Conversation* on how the pandemic produced millions more disabled people in the United States because of the rates of long COVID. In it, I mention the need for adequate funding of the SSA to meet the needs of more disabled people. I discussed the piece with a family member, and his response was, "What you're writing is good, but I would hate to see people take advantage of a bunch of money funneled into this."

I asked for further clarification because I did not understand. Indeed, what he meant was: If we fund the SSA better in order to support those with long COVID, people will find this out and fraudulently try to obtain those funds. He is an extraordinarily kind person saying something that I think for most people sounds rather unremarkable. The thing is, we don't tend to recognize this kind of sentiment as ableist because these kinds of ideas have been normalized as reasonable concerns. But they express a mix of our deeply ingrained denial of our own bodies and their inevitable need for care, as well as the false belief that there are marauding groups out there who revel in being "dependent" and gleefully steal scarce resources. These present-day assumptions stem directly from the rhetoric of eugenics.

Disability scholar Ellen Samuels writes about the long history of suspecting fakery when it comes to disability, dubbing this purportedly rampant phenomenon the "disability con." Building upon this, legal scholar Doron Dorfman notes that "news stories and memes about falsely claiming disability rights abound." To show that the fear of the disability con is still a present issue, he uses the example of a popular meme of a woman in a wheelchair who can stand for a moment being derided, along with other examples. In addition to those with varying impairments, people with invisible disabilities are particularly disparaged both online and in the world; we often require disability to be visible or identifiable in specific ways in order for it to be deemed "valid."

Given the SSA's own data, though, the fear of the disability con is far more rampant than any actual con. It's commonly assumed that disabled people receive plenty of benefits to cover their needs, that benefits are easy to get, and that fraud is widespread. But the reality is much different. The average benefit from the SSA is arguably not even a livable amount and is subject to ongoing asset tests. If you amass more than a certain amount of money, the benefit will be taken away. If it's a con, it's a very time-consuming one that likely won't even work, and if it does, still won't yield a livable income.

Ángel and Kim were lucky. He was approved on his first application. Within six months or so, Ángel started receiving his monthly SSDI checks. They were about $1,759 a month because he had so many work credits. For the moment, they could breathe a sigh of relief, but it was still not much to live on.

CHAPTER 5

Better Friends Than People

AFTER THE STROKE, ÁNGEL AND KIM MOVED TO A SMALL bungalow in a retirement community, not too far from their previous home. It has winding streets lined with nearly identical houses. Tiny lampposts dot the front of each house, and golf carts are parked in many of the driveways. When people drive down the street in their carts, they wave to each other.

Since the complex is what's called a 55-plus community, it surprised them that most of it was not built to be accessible. Luckily, their house is an outlier, with wider doorways than the others. Kim also noted to me that none of the community's four swimming pools have lifts for wheelchairs. Kim guesses that 55-plus communities like these are meant for people who will not age into disability—or at least think they won't. Maybe that's why it's called a community for "active" seniors, as though disability would disqualify one from being considered "active." In a way, the inaccessibility of this space, I supposed, is aspirational.

They were able to purchase the house because they didn't have to pay the down payment, thanks to a VA home-buying assistance benefit Ángel could access. On weekday mornings, Kim worked her new part-time job. Through a grant-funded

AARP program focused on retraining low-income workers over the age of fifty-five, she got a job doing office work for the city. She is paid Florida's minimum wage, which had recently increased from $8.56 an hour to $10.00 an hour. The pay isn't great, but the part-time hours are good. This way, Ángel doesn't have to be left alone for too long. There have been falls, including one that shattered the TV, and times when he's had to lie on the floor until she gets home. The less time alone, the better.

While Kim is out at work, she worries about him. Sometimes she has panic attacks. It will kind of hit her, there's a freeze and a stare, her heart pumping. When this happens, she'll tell her coworker, who will tell her it's okay. Everything is okay. Even though Ángel is at home safe, she worries; she still sees him in that hospital room, slipping away, still sees him that day they had to call the ambulance. In the relative calm of the new day-to-day the couple have managed to figure out, her mind and body are still grappling with the horror of what she had to see before.

At home, Ángel still wakes up early, before the sun is up. Before long, with the smell of coffee in the air, the rising sun streams through their large living-room window, backlighting Ángel. He likes to sip his coffee and sit at his usual perch, an old brown recliner in the far corner of the living room, that gives him a line of sight to most of the small house. He wears a pair of loose shorts and a T-shirt, and his glasses. In the chair, a small pillow is wedged into his left side. He periodically reaches his right hand across his body to pick up his left arm and set it back on the pillow when it falls off. This helps to keep his shoulders even, preventing his left side from slumping.

"All I do is take resources," he tells me. "I don't contribute anything." Tears stream down his cheeks as he says this. In our conversation, he repeatedly refers to himself as a "waste," lamenting how he is always just "sitting around."

He has expectations, as he describes it, for himself. He should be productive. He should be contributing financially. The responsibility for his family stops with him because, as Ángel stresses to me, he is responsible as the man of the household, unlike his experience with his father growing up. Therefore, he shouldn't just "take." Not working is at odds with his notion of what being a man means.

He feels so worthless that he questions the choice the doctors made in saving him when he coded that day in the hospital. He has even said to Kim, "Maybe you shouldn't have fought so hard to keep me, maybe you should have just let me go. Your life would've been so much easier."

Yes, he admits, that's a dark thing to say. Certainly, she would have had to mourn him. But he thinks that at least then she could have moved on with her life and not been stuck caring for him. She's young, she's vibrant, and he feels she doesn't deserve to be "burdened with the stress of me."

He seemed to reconsider what he was saying in real time. Okay, so maybe it's not that they should have just let him die, maybe it's that Kim shouldn't have brought him home. Maybe he should just be warehoused in a nursing home somewhere; then, he said, at least she wouldn't have to deal with this.

But later on that day during my visit, things took a turn.

"I'd like to mount this new striker plate on the front door," Ángel told me after lunch. We were in his living room and Kim was still at work. As he talked, he transferred himself from his recliner to his wheelchair and leaned over to pick up a small metal striker plate along with a roll of painter's tape from a side table. Using his right foot, he turned around and propelled his wheelchair toward the front door. Then he propped the roll of tape between his knees to pull off a section. He set the striker plate on the tape, pulled a little more while bracing it with his knee, and tore it off. Ángel wheeled in closer to the frame and lifted the tape and striker plate onto the inside of the door jamb, pressing it into place. It stayed there, mounted to the spot where he needed it.

"Now, I just need to screw it on." He wheeled back across the living room, got a screw from the table, and came back and passed it through the hole in the striker plate into the hole already drilled into the door jamb. "See?" Now, he was set up to use the screwdriver with his "good hand."

Earlier that morning, Ángel had announced that he had become worthless because of his disability, but now he was showing me ingenious methods for getting things done around the house, something all disabled people must do to create a habitable world. I followed him around, frantically taking notes and filming him, thinking he needed his own YouTube channel. As I watched, I remembered the ways that J and I repurposed regular household objects, just like Ángel. Like that time J and I had gone on a trip and needed to get inventive to meet her care needs. We had packed the tubing, saline bag, and bag of antifungal medicine that I regularly gave her through her chest port. Once at our hotel, we realized we didn't have an IV pole to hang the bags from. You have to hang them up high for gravity to pull the solution through the line. As a workaround, I pulled a shoestring from her boot and ran it through the holes in the tops of the clear plastic bags. They squished in my hands as I slid them on the string. Then I balanced carefully on the edge of the tub to tie it around the curtain rod. We hung out in the bathroom for a while, until the infusion had finished.

I had forgotten about this shoestring moment, but I remembered it now as I was standing there watching Ángel show me his hacks, and how he uses tools in new, unexpected ways, completely redefining their purpose. Having spoken to so many other people who shared their hacks with me, I am convinced that this is a divinely generative aspect of disability. Being misaligned with the world around you requires figuring out different, more expansive ways of being and doing. We are all just creatures seeking to move through our world in the best ways we know. In an inaccessible world, it is disabled people who often yield new, ingenious ways of doing things. In these moments, the purpose of an object might be completely, and ingeniously, reinvented. Disabled people are world builders, makers, tinkerers.

Though Ángel can no longer work as a house painter or handyman, he wants to keep figuring out how to do things. Key to this is his collection of tools and other objects that might have a use—wood chisel, putty knife, paint scraper, power sander. Many tools fill the shelves in his garage, but some of his favorites he keeps right next to him, so he can reach them from his favorite chair. Among them are the power screwdriver, painter's tape, and a clipboard with paper and pen (when you don't have a second hand to hold a piece of paper still to write on it, a clipboard is a godsend).

"Tools are better friends than people," he told me. "Some of them I've had for twenty, thirty years."

Ángel prefers spending time with his tools to socializing anyway. His friends from work disappeared once he had his stroke; he never saw any of them again. His tools and his creativity, along with Kim and his son, sustain him.

"I'm slightly more accepting of what I have no control

over . . . although I'm still very impatient with a lot of things."
Mostly, he wills himself to look at how he must do things
differently. "I try not to—consciously try not to—look at things
the way I used to do them, but rather the way I have to do
them now. I don't have a left arm, I don't have a left leg, I need
something else to work in place of them, and that's how I have
to approach doing things." Ángel has to reengineer things as
he goes.

Take dishwashing. Kim does the cooking, but he helps
with cleanup. He rolls up to the sink, gets the water soapy, and
dips the sponge in with his right hand. Then he sets the sponge
down on the countertop. Its wetness creates a suction, so it stays
put on the counter. He picks up pieces of silverware from the
sink and rubs them on the sponge, in a scrub technique that he
can do one-handed.

To bring things around the house with him while moving
around in the wheelchair, he devised a little trailer to pull along
behind him. He took a flat wooden dolly, screwed a rubber tub
on top of it, and then used rope to tie it to the chair. Because
he can't use his "good" hand to wheel the chair and carry something at once, it's a great way of transporting this.

In the garage, I noticed a series of paint sticks lining the
uneven lip from the garage floor to the driveway. When I asked
him about it, he explained that the drop of the lip was too severe
for his wheelchair, it could send him flying. So he put the sticks
down to lessen the drop. It works.

But not everything he tries works. There was an . . . *incident*.
Ángel once really wanted to slice a tomato, but had no way to
keep that thing still so he could cut it, no second hand to hold
it down. He got out his squeeze clamp and tried to secure the
tomato to the countertop. The result was one very smashed and
very messy tomato.

When Kim got home, we all sat down for dinner. We talked about how people don't ever think of disability as generating knowledge, as a culture, as something that comes with expertise and, if you want, community. It's not often thought of as a site for rethinking the purpose of everyday objects to make them work for you.

"It's just how society treats you," Ángel said.

"It's up to you to adapt, not for us to adapt to you," Kim finished.

I begin to think of Ángel as a master tinkerer. Someone who, through having a stroke, acquired knowledge, indeed useful expertise. What about all those kids out there with a disability like cerebral palsy who, like Ángel, only have use of one side? What if they wanted to build things and Ángel could teach them how? I was serious about the YouTube channel. I told Ángel as much, that I think it's all pretty genius.

"I stumbled into a bucket and came out smelling like a rose," he answered, and we all cackled. I was sitting across from them in the living room. Ángel was back in his recliner, the table with tools was next to him, and Kim was sitting in a chair beside him. As we chatted, my eyes were drawn to the carpet, where their socked feet were touching, their toes wiggling together.

One afternoon, years later, Kim texted me, "Today, we danced! I helped him stand, wrapped his left arm around my neck, and he wrapped his right arm around my waist. I laid my head on his chest with my arms around his back to hold him up, and we swayed together like the teenagers we once were."

PART II

Division of Labor

I was always ashamed to take. So I gave.
It was not a virtue. It was a disguise.
—ANAÏS NIN, *THE DIARY OF ANAÏS NIN,*
VOLUME IV (1944–1947)

CHAPTER 6

Funny Gay Males

FIRST CAME THE FALSE ALARM. IN 1995, SETH WOKE UP feeling strange. His heart was racing and his chest felt weird. He fumbled through his wallet, found his insurance card, and clutched it tightly in his hands. Then he began to pace around the bedroom, trying to think of what to do. In came his partner, Marty.

"Why are you pacing with your insurance card?" he asked, perplexed.

"I think I'm having a heart attack," Seth answered. He had wanted to handle it on his own and not bother Marty. Too late.

Luckily, it turned out not to be a heart attack after all. At the hospital, the doctor asked Seth, "Do you have any stress in your life?"

Seth explained that he was currently the healthcare proxy for his best friend, managing his care as he was dying of AIDS and . . . well, he thought, there it was: that must be the source of stress.

The mild cardiac episode was chalked up to anxiety, but Seth was still admitted for observation. Lying on a gurney in the hallway, waiting to be transferred to his floor, an orderly stared back and forth between Marty and Seth, trying to discern their relationship. This was the mid-1990s, a couple of decades before gay marriage was nationally legalized, and there was a typical lack of imagination about the existence of gay couples.

The orderly finally turned to Marty and said, "Don't worry, your dad's going to be just fine."

"I'm sorry, what did you say?" Marty asked.

"I said, don't worry, your dad is going to be just fine."

At this, Marty leaned over to Seth and said, "Did you hear that, Dad? You're going to be just fine!"

They both roared with laughter.

Seth wore a heart monitor home and was told to write a short note in a diary whenever his heart rate went up, describing what was going on at the time in order to identify potential stressors. "So, I put down, it's because my partner was an asshole—*and by the way*, I'm fifteen months younger than him!"

This time, I roared with them.

"There's always humor!" Seth said to me, smiling widely.

It was the summer of 2021, and we were sitting together in the couple's den, looking out at a handsomely manicured backyard. Theirs was a modest but well-tended home, located in a quiet suburb of New Jersey. A dogwood tree stood proudly out front, encircled by a small garden of seasonal flowers. Each year it bloomed in varying colors. Seth and his now-husband Marty were big on pinks, purples, and oranges. Marty didn't like yellow much.

It used to be that every year, the couple made a trek to a gardening center in a neighboring town. They liked to do plants of different colors and different heights around the dogwood, and they liked to change it up each year; sometimes it was tall gerbera daisies at the tree's base, purple vincas in the middle, and evergreen around the edge. It was a fun, artistic project for them to do together, though Seth started to defer to Marty on which flowers to plant—it was understood that he was going to be the one tending to them anyway.

When they first moved in, Seth, who has a degree in ornamental horticulture, had said to Marty, "I'll do the outside, you do the inside." But that agreement quickly disintegrated. Seth was apparently unwilling to move the sprinkler around the lawn throughout the day, and Marty, unable to abide unevenly watered areas, found himself traipsing across the lawn again and again to do it himself. The running joke was that Marty was doing this under duress, but Seth kept saying to him, "Well, you must like it because you keep doing it!"

———

They first met at a club nearby in 1990. Seth wasn't normally a club kind of person, but his roommate had convinced him to go with him to see a Funny Gay Males comedy show. There weren't any seats in the venue, so everyone stood to watch the show. Seth was standing in the crowd when he saw Marty arrive, looking quite dapper: shoes matching his sweater, nice pants, looking very put together indeed. Seth thought he was handsome, but Marty was talking to someone else, so he assumed they were together.

But Marty was not with anyone else, and he had seen Seth too. He strode across the floor and stood next to Seth for the duration of the show. Marty, in turn, was struck by Seth's profile: *He must be Greek, with that gorgeous straight nose!* he thought. And to Marty's surprise and pleasure, Seth kept looking over at him whenever a joke hit, laughing, as if to say, *This is hilarious, right?*

When the show was over, they started talking and quickly learned how many connections there already were between them; they were friends with some of the same people, exes, and other acquaintances. In fact, Marty had heard complaints about Seth from his ex-boyfriend. But all Marty could think was that the ex's complaints (Seth was too busy caring for others through his volunteer work, for example) were about things that sounded like admirable qualities that Marty desired in a partner.

They scheduled a date. Seth didn't have much time off between work and volunteering, and Marty wanted to maximize their time together. So they planned a day trip to an antiques mall with art galleries and cafés, with plenty of room to stroll and chat, where they could peruse and stop and eat when hungry. Although they are nearly the same age, Marty is slight in build, while Seth is taller, stockier. Seth is also generally more boisterous, Marty the less outgoing one. As they talked that day, however, they discovered similar experiences in their upbringings. They're both Jewish, and have similar values and work ethics. Both of them described their families as dysfunctional and didn't really have relationships with their siblings.

Seth had grown up in the Philadelphia area with a gifted older brother, a musical prodigy who started playing the piano at age two. Even though Seth was the younger sibling, he found himself in more of a caregiver role in the family. Seth was so good at caregiving that his nickname was Cinderfella.

This meant that Seth often had to pay attention to the family dynamics, understanding others' point of view, mediating whenever his parents had a fight, while his brother was either not around or in his room, kept out of the fray, so as not to be bogged down with any of it. His grandmother, who lived just around the corner, was a lifeline for him. He loved her and spent a lot of time with her, marveling at her tenacity and strength even as she aged. As he came of driving age, he'd pick her up for errands and the like. She would call him by the Yiddish nickname nanika schlepper because Seth was always driving older family members places they needed to go.

No surprise, then, that as an adult, Seth founded a group at his synagogue that took care of ill people. When the AIDS crisis hit and many gay men with the disease were abandoned by the state, their families, and broader culture, he was on the front lines of collective queer community care. Seth was good at all of it: wiping the patients, cleaning them, doing wound care, holding their hand, encouraging them to write down their wishes. The hands-on body care didn't bother him, and it seemed like he could handle the emotional toll as well. He began to train other volunteers.

Although he had gotten his first degree in flower care that would lead him to say that he'd tend the gardens of his and Marty's home, Seth decided to go back to school to become a vet tech in the late '90s and graduated in 2000. He had always wanted to do animal nursing; unlike people, he told me, you care for animals and they will give you unconditional love back.

Marty grew up on Long Island, the youngest by several years of three. His brother and sister were so much older they didn't have much to do with him. His father was always emotionally distant, but he was close to his mother. She was supremely organized, knew exactly where everything was, and had everything accounted for. He loved watching how, in a very precise manner, she counted out the cash for the bills each week and put it in separate envelopes for the butcher and others.

In grade school, his teacher noted Marty's special skills in math. She told him that he was a mathematical genius. He came home and proudly told his mother. From then on, he was drawn to solving problems and finding solutions, always searching for the answers. He majored in accounting in college, loving how you could find your way to a balance. "Debits had to equal credits. Things have to tie out. If something was wrong, you would know it and could work on it until you found where the error was."

Marty moved to an area near Philadelphia over a decade before that night at the comedy show. Until he met Seth, he hadn't met anyone he'd want to spend his life with. Seth was kind, funny, tough, and just so capable. There was probably something too about how whimsically Seth moved through the world, relative to Marty's buttoned-down self. When Seth lost a bracelet Marty had given him, he turned over a glass in the cupboard and prayed to St. Anthony, saying it'll turn up. Meanwhile, when Marty learned the bracelet was lost, he systematically retraced every step of Seth's, and after a couple of hours of methodically searching, found it. "Maybe next time you should pray to St. Marty instead!" he told Seth.

Marty also admired how committed Seth was to caring for other people, because *he* was definitely not as comfortable with any kind of caregiving role. Just a couple of years after meeting Seth, Marty's mother fell and broke her hip, and it was the first time Marty had to spend time in a hospital. Just walking down the hallway to her room, he became dizzy and nauseous and started to sweat. He thought he would pass out. Bodily concerns just weren't in his wheelhouse. He couldn't help it.

But make no mistake, he was not helpless. Marty had different, equally essential strengths. He told me how vulnerable his mother had become in the hospital, and how important it was for him to be her advocate during that time. Asleep in her hospital bed, an orderly once brought her a tray of food and left it. Half an hour later, the orderly came back and tried to take it away, but she was still sleeping. Marty stopped him. "Why would you take that? She hasn't had a chance to eat yet!"

His father seemed shocked that you could speak to health-care professionals that way. But Marty could not understand how the people tasked with caring for his mother could be so thoughtless. The "process improvement" person in him—that became his profession, improving processes for a pharmaceutical company—was horrified, and so he spoke up to make it better.

In 1991, less than a year after their first date, Marty and Seth moved into the house we were now sitting in decades later, just down the road from where they'd first met. They were both in their sixties. The house had pastel walls, and there were shelves and cases and tables of tchotchkes everywhere, their home filled with evidence of their life together. On one of the two sofas in the den was a throw pillow with a print made of a photo of the couple in white button-up shirts and red bow ties, smiling wide at the camera and holding their small dog, Riley, a Chiweenie, a cross between a dachshund and chihuahua, between them.

As we spoke, Seth, wearing a polo shirt, glasses, and a stack of colorful bracelets on his wrists, giggled at Riley, who was striking what they called his prairie dog pose: sitting up on his hind legs with his arms up waiting for a belly scratch. Marty sat next to them, in shorts, a hoodie, and a baseball cap, cracking jokes and telling me about a stand-up routine he is working on. After all these years together, they tell stories in an intimate choreography, each filling in where the other stops, together weaving a tale punctuated regularly by quips, and of course there is always laughter.

CHAPTER 7

On High Alert

IN 2008, MORE THAN A DECADE AFTER THAT INITIAL SCARE, Seth again experienced minor chest pain and arm soreness. It was like a dull ache that started in the morning and lasted throughout the day. He didn't think much of it at first, given the false alarm before, but this time it persisted. Just to be sure, Marty took him to the hospital and Seth had blood work done.

"So, when did you have your heart attack?" the doctor asked once the results were in. Marty and Seth looked at each other.

"I didn't think I'd ever had one," Seth answered.

"Oh, yes you did." The blood work showed high levels of a protein indicating that what he'd experienced that morning had indeed been a heart attack. Three arteries were 100 percent blocked and one was 90 percent blocked. He urgently needed open heart surgery. Hearing this news, Seth could feel the world sliding into the vortex of a new reality—and Marty would be The One to slide with him.

The next day, Seth had a quadruple bypass. The surgery went well, but his weeks of aftercare were awful. At fifty-two, he was the youngest person on the cardiac floor where he did much of his recovery. The doctors had told him a typical post-surgical stay was five to seven days, and that with his relative youth, it would all be fine. But Seth ended up staying in the hospital for nearly three weeks.

Marty had unexpectedly lost his job just a few weeks prior to Seth's surgery, leaving him with time to be at the hospital with Seth. He immediately committed to making the process as excellent as it could be for Seth, but to do so, he had to face his fear of hospitals and had to confront human bodies, their fluids and their corporeal problems. It was his worst nightmare. And it didn't help that the hospital was not known as the best; it was old, dreary, in general disrepair. When Marty first trudged across the street from the parking lot to the building and up the steps, there was scaffolding and construction. Inside, he navigated hallways obscured by tarps, all adding to the unpleasantry of what he was going through now.

When Marty got to the critical care unit where Seth was convalescing immediately after surgery, "He looked like a cadaver," Marty told me. Seth was intubated, lying in the bed with an abundance of tubes snaking out of his body, collecting fluids from him in bags alongside the bed. Marty's stomach turned and that old wooziness snuck up on him again. He had to look away. This was his partner, the love of his life, but how was he to be The One to take care of him if he wasn't even capable of being in the same room without averting his eyes? But Marty could not escape the feeling that if he just made all the best choices, then things would turn out okay for Seth. And Seth being okay was all that mattered. Marty tried to focus his mind: What were the next steps and how would they move through them so that this would all be over?

He paid close attention, but he was overwhelmed: "I wasn't able to process the information, the dribs and drabs I was getting from nurses." Eventually, he brought in legal pads to keep notes because "I realized I wasn't retaining anything, and I needed to write everything down." It had all happened so fast. Marty was on his own, couldn't make sense of it, and couldn't confer with the one person he normally conferred with on everything. Even when Seth was no longer intubated and had regained consciousness, Marty still had to watch his partner lying there with tubes and IVs coming everywhere out of his body.

After days of a seemingly endless parade of different doctors coming to see Seth, Marty drew a chart to try to get his arms around everything, to understand the big picture. He took down the title and information of every provider that visited, building out an organizational chart. "Hospitals have teams, then there's hospital staff, then there are providers who aren't employees of the hospital, they would come in too . . . round and round and no one identifying what team they were from." His head was spinning.

Most worrying to Marty was that he didn't know what he was supposed to be watching for. How would they know if Seth was doing well? Or worse, that he wasn't?

"I was just there to try to prevent mistakes," Marty said. "You have to stay on top of the hospital staff. There are too many patients, not enough providers. And everyone might be disjointed and not communicating. When you're the caregiver, you're the one node that connects them all together, particularly if your loved one is not able to (nor should they have to!) navigate all of this. They may be out of it, they may be in pain, they may be in their own trauma about what is happening to them. How can we expect them to stay on top of their care to the degree that it might be needed?"

As Marty told me this part of his story, my own memories of J's hospitalizations unspooled inside me. Marty was articulating what it is like when your loved one is in the hospital, and you feel it is your job to make sure all the best decisions are made. I recognized the overwhelming complexities of the healthcare system he was describing—dealing with the various and often

not-communicating-with-each-other departments, the person-
nel shift changes, the electronic records, the sheer wonder of
medical technology as well as its mind-boggling, labyrinthine
processes and procedures. To healthcare workers who are on the
front lines all day every day, these things may be routine, even
unremarkable. But for those of us who are The One, each detail,
each process, and each fact about the healthcare system feels
like life or death for the person we love.

When J was hospitalized, the number of departments involved in her care made my head spin: dermatology, the transplant
team, cardiology, physical therapy, endocrinology, infectious
diseases, pulmonology, and on and on. During her transplant, I
instinctively and obsessively tracked everything: her daily blood
counts, her kidney function, urine output, the size, shape, and
texture of a rash, the number of bowel movements. Like Marty,
the best way for me to get through our reality was to write everything down in a notebook, to keep a history.

I did this to be on top of J's care, but also to perform competence and, in some way, worth. I endeavored to be useful,
sharing information as a way to develop relationships with
the nurses and various professionals involved with her care.
Maybe if they saw me as a person, saw J as a person, and us
as a couple—a real couple with feelings and a life together—
maybe she would get better care. I was ingratiating, but I did
it because I thought it could save J's life.

I regularly sneaked out of the room while J was sleeping
in the hopes of catching a nurse at her station. "Just wanted
to check in!" I would say brightly. I learned to casually talk
counts, infusing my words with an affect that suggested a
shared professional curiosity. I didn't want to seem like yet
another burdensome family member of a patient. I thought I
could render the hospital staff more amenable to my queries if

I could somehow be "one of them," talking with them rather than seen as someone asking for more of their labor. "Are we trending up or trending down?" I would say, mirroring language I had heard them use previously, to show them that I could handle the discourse. I was afraid of not being taken seriously because of our queerness or young age. (We were in our twenties, after all.) I would tell them I was a PhD student in sociology, specializing in medical sociology. I asked them to please explain things to me thoroughly. *Give it to me real.*

As an educated white woman advocating for J, I leveraged privileges that others are not given. Decades of research show disparities in how people are treated in medicine. It is well documented that Black and other patients of color routinely receive poorer medical care. As award-winning sociologist and cultural critic Dr. Tressie McMillan Cottom writes, Black women are especially ignored, viewed only as "incompetent" and not listened to about their care needs. Myths about Black people having higher pain tolerances than white people have long been perpetuated, along with similar myths about Indigenous and other people of color, all of which results in less safety and worse care for people of color in the healthcare context. That is to say, patient advocacy is needed more in some situations than in others. And in my role as The One, I had already been given a head start.

I rattled off blood count trends and med dosages during doctors' rounds. I was good at it; I could pull out of my head the numbers from the day before, the week before. I had it all right there in my recall, as well as in my notebooks. I freely gave my intimate knowledge of what meds typically worked for J and which ones didn't and why. I was extra careful to know which meds might be contraindicated by others, checking, making sure, *did they know that she had a bad reaction to that med last time?* I believed I had something akin to expertise—even if my expertise was of J and her body, not a general medical expertise per se—and my goal was to demonstrate it so I could be taken seriously.

While all this was a strategy to ensure that J got the best care possible, it was also how I mitigated my own terror of her death. I had to think that my knowledge could at least give J some kind of advantage, no matter how slight. I could not bear the loss of her; what if I missed something and that caused her to die?

On the transplant floor of Memorial Sloan Kettering in 2006, just two years before Marty and Seth found themselves in the hospital in New Jersey for the second time, I remember an endless cycle of masks and gowns donned to go in and out of the rooms. It was a special floor with special rules for patients without functioning immune systems. Every night, the light of the New York City skyline seemed to pour in through the windows at a slant—or maybe it was just my world that was askew.

"I wish I could kiss you," J said, from behind her surgical mask.

Our breaths were tinged with the smell of reverse filtrated hospital air.

"You can have all the paper kisses you want," I said, behind my own mask.

———

One person on the surgical team seemed to connect with Marty, so Marty asked him to take him through everything step-by-step. The doctor kindly went through all the things that needed to happen in order for Seth to be released. Marty made a list and held on to it for dear life. But Seth did not seem to be hitting these milestones. In fact, Marty had to stand by and watch as Seth acquired significant edema, swelling up with so much water weight that he couldn't walk, couldn't get out of bed, couldn't toilet.

"He's young, he'll recover, he'll be fine," the doctors kept telling Marty. But the edema was astounding. And despite a revolving door of different providers and teams coming into and out of the room at all hours of the day, no one seemed to notice that things were not good. Physical therapy kept coming, but the edema was now so severe that Seth could barely move. Marty was terrified and frustrated. Seth was immobilized.

One day, about a week after surgery, Marty left the room for a few moments. "When I came back—and I was gone from the room maybe five minutes tops—a doctor was on his way out. I said, 'Did you examine Seth?' He said, 'Oh, yes, he's doing fine.'"

Marty stood there, stunned. He wondered how the doctor could possibly have had time to conduct the exam in the brief moments Marty was out of the room.

The next day, on Sunday, the same doctor returned. This time, Marty was there. The doctor palpated Seth's ankles, he felt his wrists, saw that he had edema, but said to Seth, "You're doing fine. Do you have any questions for me?"

Marty certainly did.

"When was Seth's surgery?"

"I don't know, it would be in the chart."

"If you don't know when Seth's surgery was, how do you know he's doing fine? Is he doing fine for somebody who just got out of surgery? It's ten days postsurgery, and I don't think that's doing fine."

"I have thirty patients; you can't expect me to know the condition of every one of my patients," the doctor answered.

Marty gritted his teeth. He inquired when Seth would be well enough to go home.

The doctor said, "He'll go home when we say he can go home."

———

After Marty's disappointing conversation with the physician, Seth was seen by a fourth cardiologist. And when Marty said a *fourth*, I thought again about how complex healthcare delivery is. Whether inpatient or outpatient, healthcare in America is complex and fragmented for many reasons. One reason is because of something called "managed care," which was first associated with prepaid health plans called HMOs, or health maintenance organizations. The term was coined in 1970 to describe how insurance companies form groups to manage costs. Then, in 1973, the Health Maintenance Organization Act "provided a major impetus to the expansion of managed health care. . . . The purpose of the legislation was to stimulate greater competition within health-care markets . . . [It] marked an important turning point in the U.S. health-care industry because it introduced the concept of for-profit health-care corporations to an industry long dominated by a not-for-profit business model."

The turn to managed care solidified our inverted relationship to healthcare consumption in the United States. Run as a business, the priority would always be cost savings, which can be at odds with providing the best care. This shift also occurred while neoliberalism (characterized by decreased funding for the public sector in favor of privatization) began to dominate our economic policies: "The pivotal forces propelling the movement to managed care in the 1980s were financial, namely, reduced government support for public sector health care and escalating costs in the private sector. . . . Managed care is not about managing care—but about managing costs or competition."

Since managed care changed the structure of healthcare delivery, it also changed patients' individual experience of it. Patients, and therefore their caregivers, may experience it now in the purchasing of small hospitals by private equity firms, the spiraling out of more and more specializations, and the crisscrossing of teams and services hired from outside hospitals or clinics, further complicating and fracturing the care we receive by outsourcing it because it may be cheaper. When you have such a complex care-delivery system focused on profits, there is, among other things, more and more care to coordinate and fewer paid employees to provide the care and coordination that is needed. And here is where we find Marty and Seth.

When the fourth cardiologist came in, picked up Seth's chart, and flipped through it, Marty was on high alert.

Reviewing the records, the doctor noted Seth's weight and Marty said, "That can't possibly be right."

"Why not?" the doctor asked.

"That's seventeen pounds heavier than when he came in," Marty explained. "The first two days he was intubated, and he hasn't really been eating, so how could he be seventeen pounds heavier?"

"It's probably the edema," the cardiologist said.

"Is seventeen pounds normal?" Marty asked. "Because that seems like an enormous amount. And the physical therapist is coming in, and she can't get him to do his physical therapy, and he can't walk. I'm assuming it's because of the edema. Shouldn't we be addressing this? Shouldn't this be the first thing?"

Marty said all this, but inside, he blanched. "This is me speaking to a cardiologist," he told me. "I know nothing, I'm just trying to advocate for Seth."

The cardiologist answered, "Well, we are giving him a diuretic."

"Yes, but should you be bumping it up? It's seventeen pounds."

"Things will take time. Everybody's body is different."

"It's been ten days."

"If you increase the diuretic, he could go into kidney failure. We don't want to do that."

"Obviously," Marty said. "Does that happen instantaneously, or are there signs that you're going into kidney failure?"

"There are signs. It would show up in blood work, and we are doing blood draws twice a day. I see where you're going with this. Yes, it would make sense that we increase the diuretic," the physician decided, thanks to Marty's advocacy.

They doubled the diuretic, Lasix, and Seth dropped seven pounds the first night, which made him more comfortable. Things were looking up. At least something was improving, something was working. The couple felt hopeful.

But then came the run-in with a substitute nurse who had been borrowed from a different hospital to cover a shift.

Because Seth had so much edema after the surgery, a port was put in. A port is surgically placed under the skin, and has a "drum" and a catheter, the latter of which is threaded into a vein, making blood draws and med deliveries easier. Seth's port was placed in his chest, near the clavicle, and he had a drip line continuously running into it, keeping it open and clean. They used this line for his daily labs.

But that morning, the per diem nurse unhooked Seth's IV from the chest port so she could help him toilet. She then left the port unhooked, thinking that perhaps it would be better for Seth to be able to go to the bathroom on his own throughout the day. She would manually flush the line later, she said.

As a licensed animal nurse and long-time vet tech, Seth had some medical knowledge, and he knew that she needed to either reconnect it or flush it or the line would close. If a port isn't kept "open" by regularly flushing it with fluids, the blood clots and begins to block the line, rendering it useless. "I was out of it," Seth told me, so he didn't catch it. This time, neither did Marty.

The nurse never came back. She never reconnected the drip into the port. She never manually flushed it. When it came time to draw blood for labs that night, the line no longer worked. The nurses alerted the doctors.

The doctor there that night was a resident, a doctor who was still completing his training under the supervision of an attending physician in a particular specialty, in this case cardiac surgery. He came to Seth's room and said he would have to put in a new port. Marty has never forgiven himself for what happened to Seth next.

CHAPTER 8

The Blue Gloves

MARTY WAS GONE BY THE TIME IT HAPPENED. WHEN THE resident came back, it was late, after visiting hours were over, around 10:00 p.m. Skin stretched and body bloated with edema underneath the paper-thin hospital gown, tired and uncomfortable from all the tubes, the round-the-clock beeping, the traffic of the hospital floor—desperate for his heart to beat, to breathe without pain, to be back in the body he had always known—Seth was now tilted down in his hospital bed, inverted so that his head was lowered and his feet were up. His head ached with the pressure.

While inverted and powerless, the resident pulled the old port out of his recently sewn chest. The long catheter that had snaked through his jugular artery slicked out, and the result was bloody and wet. Then, the resident began mucking around to try to correctly place the new port. Usually, this would be done with numbing and ultrasound guidance. But not this time.

For the next two hours, Seth, who describes himself as someone with a very high pain tolerance, began to understand that this resident was jabbing the catheter in all the wrong places; it felt like Seth's bones, his clavicle, his sternum were being stabbed with a knife. All of this he felt acutely, because he experienced it without anesthesia or pain medication. As the resident continued to try to place the port and thread the catheter, Seth's mind made the decision to leave.

There was a fluorescent light on the ceiling above him. It bothered his eyes, but it also washed out everything around him. He could no longer perceive anything aside from his vague awareness of the blue gloves the doctor and nurses were wearing—the color of a robin's egg. They stood over him talking. He rose above himself, hovering somewhere near the light; there was only "the brightness of the light and the hands all over me." And the pain.

At one point, a plastic part of the port bent. The resident had only brought one port, so there was a long wait for another one to arrive. Seth could sense the resident's irritation that it wasn't working. "I was trying not to say anything, not to tell them how painful it was because I just wanted them to be able to do it."

All the while, he was still tilted upside down.

While relaying this story to me, Seth was suddenly transported. "It was all so painful, very painful. Because you could feel them pulling up and pushing down, and the wire . . . it was in my neck, but he kept hitting bone." I watch his eyes dart, his shoulders clench. "Let's stop and take a deep breath," I told him.

When Marty looks back on this time, this day is *the* big memory for him. "That's the thing I still beat myself up about . . . in the afternoon, I should have insisted she rehook him up, or I should have said, 'Did you flush him?' and I didn't. That got by me. That shouldn't have gotten by me." That night, Marty had even tried to call the doctor and ask if they could just wait until the morning, see if the decreased edema would render the port unnecessary. But this route was not taken. And it haunts Marty that he wasn't able to be there.

Seth also wonders if there was something he could have done. Maybe he should have spoken up, asked for some kind of pain medication, but he was simply too preoccupied trying to survive it. Like Marty, he beats himself up for letting it happen. After the fact, the couple did request a conversation with the head nurse. She apologized for what happened with the substitute nurse and said they wouldn't use her again. But the damage was done.

And what is there to do? What recourse does one have? Seth and Marty may not have known then that, spurred in part by patient rights movements in the 1970s and HIV/AIDS patient movements in the 1980s, the role of the patient advocate, or patient representative, emerged in hospitals to assist with a wide range of patient matters, including dissatisfaction with care.

J and I did not interface with the patient advocate much, maybe once. I recall that we felt it awkward to ask someone on the hospital staff to "investigate" or resolve some conflict we had with another hospital employee. Mostly, I recall feeling afraid someone would get mad at us and it would negatively affect J's care. It's all the more reason why patients and their families may not feel empowered to speak up. If you make waves, you can't help but worry that the people working in the hospital might get irritated and might take it out on you.

In addition to hospital-based patient advocates, industries have emerged to address these gaps in care. People can hire their own patient advocates, navigators, or care coordinators to help facilitate and optimize care. These of course require the financial resources to privately employ them. It seems we've tried to answer a negative consequence of turning healthcare into a market with yet another market. For those who can't afford such private care navigation, it can mean an even greater reliance on The One, who must add patient advocacy to their list of job titles.

Marty describes this role aptly, saying, "I felt I was always starting at square zero every third day. I was the liaison between the surgical team, the cardiology team, the hospital staff. That shouldn't be. That shouldn't be in a healthcare environment. What if Seth didn't have somebody there with a legal pad taking notes?"

Looking back, Marty and Seth speculate about if Seth's line had been unhooked and left like that because they are gay. Was it an innocent mistake? Or was this nurse homophobic? They don't know, but they can't help but wonder.

Once he was discharged, Seth spent the next year recovering, sleeping in a recliner because he couldn't lie flat, and trying to manage the pain he now lived with. Whenever it rained, the incision down his chest ached and pulled and puffed so much it incapacitated him. He availed himself of every resource for getting through it. He completed a certificate in chronic pain self-management, a six-week course that taught him how to breathe during intense pain and to "train my brain and body how to cope."

He didn't just endure physical pain, but psychic pain. Whenever he thought about the port incident, tension would shoot straight to his jaw. His whole body seemed to clench in response to the memory, but his jaw would clench so hard that his bottom teeth felt, as he put it, as though they would be "ejected" from his body.

When the night of the port came up in our conversations, even so many years later, and Seth described the resident poking his sternum, he actually felt it, as though it were happening all over again. The past is still his present, there is still unease when the topic is brought up. Then, he laughed because he told me his grandmother would have joked with him about it in Yiddish, saying that he was just having stomach issues. "But that's where it affects me." After the hospitalization, he slowly worked to absorb the full extent of what had happened to him, both in body and mind. He learned to breathe. He learned to endure the pain.

Little did he know that the cascade of another illness was coming for him, just as he was starting to feel almost "normal" again.

———

A couple of years after his heart attack, Seth was at work when he started shivering. He was wearing scrubs and sitting in the vet office. Although he had returned to work after the heart attack, it was part time and with modified duties. Instead of working full time in direct animal care, lifting larger animals and being on his feet all day—work that he had loved and that he had been good at—they had him in reception doing admin work, doling out meds, or making phone calls. But that day, something was wrong. He went home.

The next morning, he got up and padded barefoot into the bathroom to shave. When he looked down, the big toe on his right foot was entirely black.

His toe had to be amputated immediately. His blood flow was severely compromised. To treat this vascular problem, veins from one leg had to be harvested to put in the other. He spent months recovering. He had to relearn entirely how to walk, how to take steps, and how to keep his balance.

What Marty and Seth didn't know was that this was just the beginning. Seth, who had been a well-managed diabetic for decades without issues, soon developed a wound on the other foot—the one with all the toes—and later a lump formed. He got that wound treated, and the doctors sent him home with his foot wrapped up.

They went in for his checkup, expecting his foot to be doing better. But when they unwrapped it, "stuff came flying out," Seth said. "Suddenly all the insides of Seth's foot started to pour out onto the floor," Marty added. Seth could handle the gore, but Marty could not. Once again, Marty turned away, averting his eyes.

The podiatrist sent Seth to the wound center, where he was told he had Charcot foot, a rare and chronic disease.

"I'd never heard of it," Seth said. "The way it was explained to me was it has to do with your blood pressure. And I had good blood pressure, but when you have Charcot, some diabetics have a situation where blood rushes to a joint." The rush of the blood can lead to "breaks or microfractures of the bones." The bones are immediately under the skin and can puncture it, creating wounds that, because of poor blood flow, are more susceptible to infection. It means Seth is constantly battling infections in his foot, in addition to persistently having broken bones.

When Seth has a Charcot episode, it's imperative that he stay completely off his foot. This means he regularly spends weeks to months at a time in bed, only getting up to go to the bathroom. If he has a fracture, then surgery to fix it, he'll stay in bed for weeks, then graduate to a cast for months. Once he's progressed into the cast, Seth must relearn to stand, pivot, and walk in a new cast that touches the ground differently than the last cast. When he's in the casting phase, it must be monitored closely and thus looked at and recast almost weekly. It is as though he gets a new body each week that he must learn how to balance and maneuver. More than a dozen years later, Seth is still in cycle after cycle of Charcot destroying his foot.

Along the way in each round of the cycle, sometimes he picks up an infection, sometimes he doesn't. If he does, it adds an additional layer of treatment, but he eventually progresses to a custom boot, then to a custom shoe, all while using a cane.

His foot will never be "fixed," it will never go back to being what it was. Which means there is never a break, never a rest. As soon as it gets better, the cycle always begins again. He'll be okay, and then his bones will shift and fracture again and again and again.

Living in this constant wound cycle means Seth is always dealing with revolving setbacks and plateaus. He may spend weeks or months in bed, and he has to muster the mental fortitude to survive it. "I don't react well to being bedbound," Seth told me. But he does it—with the help of TV, phone calls, coloring books, podcasts, and his own mind. He doesn't want friends to see him this way. He calls them and tells them to take Marty out instead.

No longer does Seth suffer from that jaw-clenching terror from the port insertion. What haunts him the most now is his foot. He has a recurring dream that he has gone into the wound center for one of his routine appointments. But when he gets there, they tell him they must amputate his foot. He says he isn't ready, but the nurses tell him that now is the time. He struggles to get away and looks for help, but Marty isn't there. He wakes up.

CHAPTER 9

Role Reversal

NEVER-ENDING WOUND CARE IS, OF COURSE, MARTY'S greatest inability. He is still not able to handle wound changes. Seth does it entirely on his own. He sits down on the closed toilet, puts a towel down on the floor, and a hand mirror. He uses the mirror to look at the underside of his foot. It is always quite frightening; depending on the size of the wound, it can take up a third of his foot and can be so deep there is no skin, only the fatty pink pad of his sole. In the beginning he held his breath as he exposed and dressed the wound. "There were times I did it and didn't speak about it because I knew how Marty felt about it," he told me.

Once Seth removes the soiled bandage, he applies a salve or iodine to the wound, then rewraps it with tape and bandages. He does it every day for as long as it takes. Sometimes months go by as the wound gets smaller and smaller, but eventually it gets bigger and the cycle starts all over again. Though upset, Seth just sighs and starts doing his own intensive wound care again.

Marty learned quickly to stand in a certain position behind the chair Seth sits in at the wound doctor or podiatrist so he doesn't have to see it. When they look at pictures from week to week to track Seth's healing process, Marty turns away from the screen. Instead of looking he thinks about all the other things that need doing, that he will do. "I'm just not good at hands-on caregiving, anything blood or body-related," he told me.

"I know I'm not the best caregiver out there, but I'm doing an okay job and I'm trying very hard." I heard it in his voice, the exhaustion, the delicate line of trying to tell yourself that you're doing a good job but feeling like it still isn't enough and never will be. He is forever trying to forgive himself for all the things he can't do. From what happened to Seth in the hospital with the port, to anything that doesn't go exactly according to plan.

"Seth's well-being comes before my own well-being," he said. Seth's comfort is what matters to him, and to achieve that, Marty needs to do what he does best: ensuring that all the processes are intact and as efficient as possible. If he can manage this, he can keep the overwhelm at bay. But it's not easy. "It feels like what I'm doing is never enough to make things right."

While Seth endures the bodily experience of his Charcot cycles, Marty tries to manage everything else coming at them. What this division of labor means is that they are each in some way alone in their own experience. And for Marty, as The One, he is often solo in the daily matters, the chores, domestic life. Being The One often means being so busy that Marty hardly has time even to think or process what is happening or the damage it's doing to him emotionally. The demands are all just too immediate; he's the call center, the tech guy, the finance guy, and everything in between, while navigating healthcare systems, coordinating care, dealing with all the disability admin, and tracking finances.

"It's so important to admit there are times when you are completely at a loss or overcome." Yet Marty feels the weight of the expectations as Seth's partner. "Because you're the spouse you should be able to handle all of this mentally, physically, all of the demands."

Intellectually, he knows these are unrealistic expectations, but he still feels bad if he doesn't meet them. "Being a caregiver is nothing you choose to be, you're put in that position." He tries to remind himself that just because the role was forced upon you doesn't mean you have the tools or the skills to do it. There's also just not knowing how to deal with the emotional fallout, but feeling like you should. "A lot of it is just lacking the skill set of somebody who is trained, who's more capable, and yet everybody thinks, because you're the spouse you should be able to handle all of the frustration, to never get angry."

Round and round the emotions and the tasks go, looping again and again through the cycle of Charcot. To survive hospitalization, somebody has to be The One; once the stay is over, that someone is also The One navigating insurance to pay for the visit, and then everything else that unfolds in the years after.

Because of the way our systems are designed, disability admin is a never-ending job. Across the country, countless caregivers are worn down by admin tasks like insurance billing. There's an entire system's worth of work that often gets put on The One. For his part, Marty makes complex Excel spreadsheets to manage Seth's ongoing drug costs. Seth's different conditions—heart, Charcot, diabetes, etc.—means he takes a couple of dozen medications a day, requires diabetic equipment, and uses various wound-care supplies for his foot. Tracking it all and getting things covered by insurance is a whole other job.

"Each insurance company can offer multiple Medicare drug plans. Blue Cross Blue Shield could have three or four different plans in your area." He pulled up spreadsheets he's made to compare plans for the cost of each of Seth's drugs. "This first sheet is just the list of all the meds or supplies, and it lists what the cost for that is within that company, within that plan."

As I stared at the spreadsheet, my head spun. In our conversations, words like *deductibles, plan years, initial costs, cumulative costs,* and *thresholds* practically flew out of Marty's mouth. "Once they've exceeded $4,020, then you move into what's called *the hole phase.* Once the cumulative costs hit $6,350, that moves you out of the doughnut hole and into *the catastrophic phase.*"

As he talked to me about it, my eyes glazed over. What I gathered from this soup of policy-speak (a skill of Marty's I admire very much) is that depending on the phase you're in, you pay a different price. While I was still staring at the countless spreadsheets, Marty unveiled another he has devised to capture costs for each individual drug.

"Doesn't this just defy all logic?" I asked him, rubbing my temples.

"Yes. Seth keeps saying to me, 'What does the average person do?'"

———

While Marty carries the weight of these systems, Seth tries to make sense of a demoralizing disease that beats him down with its relentlessness. "What's your relationship with your foot?" I ask him.

"Hate-hate," he answered.

He joked about wanting to pick a new one up at "Foot-R-Us" and then immediately grew solemn. He said, "You wonder what you could have done to prevent it, being a mild diabetic. But there was nothing. I asked the doctor several times. He said you couldn't have, it's just genetics or whatever, but that's the kind of thing you think about."

Seth copes by silently willing himself to handle it. *Don't be a burden*, he thinks. But the fact is, he moves slowly now.

"Things take longer because of me. I used to get out of bed at five or six in the morning, take a quick five-minute shower, put my scrubs on, and go out the door. Now it's, oh, you have to wrap the cast. I have to tape it so it's waterproof. I have to sit on that shower chair. I have to handhold the shower, instead of the rain shower." He could get ready in under ten minutes before, but not anymore.

Seth tries to manage the anger and resentment that sometimes boils up. But once, when he went to pick up his keys off the table, they fell to the floor. Every expletive flew out of Seth's mouth. "I wasn't angry at the keys. I was angry at the situation." He hated being weak. He hated needing to rely on other people.

Of course, he has a long history of caring for others and has time and time again allowed others to rely on him without judgment, but when he thinks of needing help himself, he is uncomfortable with the role reversal. "It has a negative connotation for me. I have always been the one to do things for others." He was, as he put it, "groomed for this idea of not needing anything."

He keeps as much as he can inside. "If you don't tell anybody anything, you've got total control. Because when you're aging badly," he told me, "you're a burden to others." He's resentful that he and Marty are aging differently, and that he is the one aging badly, which he explains to me means that he is "negatively, physically impacting another person's life, being a weight, being an albatross."

He sees the irony here. Of how Marty had never been a

caregiver before they met, and didn't have the skills for it, or so they thought. And yet here is Seth, the one needing the care when he is most comfortable giving it.

He keeps his needs to himself as best he can, always pushing things as far as he can go on his own. His silent bearing, his will to control, is a defense mechanism, he admits. "I can tell him about the toe, but the whole leg bleeding thing I'm not going to tell him. I just wrap it up and hide it." He would even have hemorrhages, since he was on too many blood thinners, but still he hid it, at least until he finally would tell Marty he needed to be taken to urgent care.

It feels more self-sufficient to handle it all himself. He doesn't tell his friends about what he calls his "tale of woes" either. What can they do? What is there to say, and will they stick around? He feels more in control when he grits through it, flexing his mental toughness in pulling up that twenty-something, nondisabled version of himself that still exists in his mind.

When I spoke to Seth in 2021, he was holding fast to the mythical idea that if he can just control his mind, he'll overcome what is happening to his body. That if he can will himself through it, he can protect both himself, and Marty, from his needs. And this is how he plots to avoid being a burden, to lessen the stress on The One by taking the pressures and putting them on himself.

It's not just people he doesn't want to rely on; he doesn't want to rely on mobility devices either. A scooter would help him get around and do more things, but for him it is just another symbol of dependence. In Seth's mind, even though a scooter would give him "mobility without consequences," he doesn't want one. Yet with one, he could, for example, traverse a large casino all day, play the slots—one of his favorite things to do—and not experience pain. It would be freeing, he admitted, with a deep sigh.

Marty did talk him into using a scooter at a casino once. He just wanted Seth to be happy, to go to the casino and have fun because "Seth loves pushing the buttons!" And if they could just get there and use the scooter, he could enjoy himself. Nothing would give Marty more pleasure than seeing Seth happy.

Seth was able to play the slots that day. They even had a good cackle when Seth couldn't figure out the scooter controls; he was trying to park it and get out, but he kept running into the wall instead. Still, when I asked Seth about how it felt to use the scooter, he said that it made him deeply self-conscious.

"I'm thinking, 'Now I'm one of this crowd, and I don't want to be.'"

When he sees other people using scooters, he sees the looks they get. "Even though it gave me great mobility, it drew attention." He'd rather experience discomfort and not use the scooter. People will stare, he says.

"When I get in it, and I zip around and I see people looking at me, I want to say, 'I don't normally need this.' I say that in my mind. It's not to say that those other people are bad. It's that I don't want to be thought of as that bad off physically."

He recognizes this as "a prejudice" that he has. Like so many other disabled people, he tries to distance himself from being perceived as disabled. "When you see people on it, you think, 'That's not for me.' Well, it's for me now."

His relationship to disability is shaky. A few years ago at a foot appointment Seth heard his doctor casually mention that Seth had been his patient for eight years now for his "chronic illness." But he has had a hard time seeing himself that way.

More recently though, he was warming to the idea. "The way he said it this time, I heard him," Seth said. He told me that our conversations were some of the first in which he has used the words *chronic illness*.

"I would've never said that before." Instead, he would have said, "Oh, I'm just dealing with this and it flares up every once in a while."

If he were to think of himself as disabled, then he might become so. "Right now, I am just coming to terms with the fact that I have a chronic illness, but I don't think of myself as chronically ill. That's really weird because I am, but I don't think of it as that. . . . Hopefully, that's keeping me more active. . . . If I thought of myself as chronically ill, I might become that, and I don't want to become it."

CHAPTER 10

Alone Together

IN 2024, SETH AND MARTY MOVED. THEY PACKED UP THEIR house of the last few decades, saying goodbye to the one extra-tall step that led from the front porch to the front entryway, goodbye to the stairs going down to the basement, goodbye to the manicured yard and beloved garden that required so much work. Managing these things just wasn't doable anymore. They moved into an apartment: one level, no more accessibility issues.

In the fall, Seth was hospitalized for yet another infection after yet another foot surgery. But then they saw a new vascular doctor, who did an angiogram. This time, they discovered areas where blood flow in his foot was not good and were able to address them. He also had a PICC line at this point, a line inserted into the arm with a catheter up into a vein in the chest. It can be used to deliver IV medications at home. With the improved blood flow to the foot, the doctors ordered additional weeks of IV antibiotics. This would hopefully stave off infection much more effectively.

Maybe this angiogram would be the thing that would improve his blood flow and his foot's healing process, and therefore somehow make things better for Seth. It was worth a try, but Seth was weary after so many years of this.

Four years after first connecting with Marty and Seth in 2020, Seth told me that, for the first time, he was considering amputation. He had watched the 2024 Paralympics on TV over the summer. Seeing others with amputations, he felt some kind of normalization of it, a kind of opening within himself.

He asked his doctor about amputation and a prosthetic foot. His doctor was surprised. It's not that no one had mentioned this solution to Seth before, it's that this was the first time he was open to talking about it. During a visit about three years earlier, both Seth and Marty had been aghast, even offended, at the suggestion of amputation. But now, after years more of the Charcot cycle, and after watching the Paralympians, Seth sees what they can do and wonders if it might be time for him soon.

———

On a recent morning, they had to get ready for their couples therapy appointment. Marty went into Seth's room to see what he was doing. He was asleep, so Marty woke him up. They were facing some time constraints. He needed to do an infusion of an antibiotic through his PICC line, but it takes time to set up and run the infusion. Seth needed to infuse that morning because of his recent infection, so he needed to get up and do that early so they could get to their appointment on time.

"I have my infusion ready, don't worry, I'm good," Seth told Marty from bed.

Marty didn't think he looked ready, but said okay, took him at his word. He went to get ready himself. When he finished about an hour later, he went back into Seth's room and discovered that he was still fast asleep under the covers. He woke Seth up again.

"We have an appointment! We need to get to the appointment, you haven't infused!"

Seth, having just been woken up, began cursing and yelling at Marty to leave him alone. He was not in a good mood. He was over this body and every little setback, all the things that just kept happening to him. He was frustrated. "This shit has to stop, I can't take this anymore!"

Marty felt horrible, not just because Seth was so upset but also because in the end, Seth was not able to infuse before the appointment, and Marty blamed himself for all the things that could now go awry.

Ever since the port incident in the hospital all those years ago, Marty has been on his own lonely mental carousel: *If I had just made a different, better choice then things would be okay.* If, when he had gone into the bedroom the first time, he had just made sure Seth was actually awake. If he had been more proactive in making sure the infusion had begun instead of letting Seth go back to sleep. If he had just not walked out, if, if if. If he had done a better job, none of this would be happening and everything would be okay.

For Seth, this argument was just another moment in the never-ending saga of his body. He can check out sometimes. He can let things go. But for Marty, his mind grips tighter and tighter.

Years and years of this chronic illness were taking their toll on them both, and on their relationship. "He's a caregiver who doesn't want to be, but he does a good job, he's a great advocate," Seth said of Marty. But the Charcot changes their relationship dynamic. "He's almost like a parent . . . and I'm a little kid, which I don't like because I'm not." Seth is constantly feeling infantilized, while Marty feels he can't *not* micromanage everything, because that's what has kept things afloat thus far.

"I don't feel like we're equals," Marty told me when we talked on our own. "I think once you become a caregiver, it almost becomes parental. I don't know if that happens in all relationships, but to me, it seems more parental. You're making a lot of the decisions that don't seem to be collaborative. That's, I think, the hardest thing."

"I'm sure he doesn't want to be the parent," Seth told me, when we had our own chance to talk about this. "But he's always looking to make sure that I'm not physically doing something that could hurt me. Even carrying in a bag from food shopping. We'll open the trunk and I'll say, 'Give me a bag.' And I have the cane. I have a bag. 'No, you shouldn't be doing that.' It's like, 'Yes, I can do it.' Yesterday, I did it and it was fine. I might fumble, I might whatever, but I do it."

Off to couples therapy they went.

At the appointment, they processed what had happened that morning, and where things stood. For now, they'll wait and see if the angiogram procedures have truly made things any better. If he amputates, there would be no more infections, no more hospitalizations. But he would lose his foot. How is he supposed to make that choice?

Marty still fixates on all the things that don't go right. He feels guilty when things aren't the best they can be for Seth. "That's just who I am, and that's a horrible trait to have as a caregiver." But he is working on it. He's trying to forgive himself.

That day, after therapy, Marty described being The One to me this way: It's "like when your parents took you to the ocean for the first time and they taught you to jump so you weren't knocked down by the wave." That's where he is right now. He sees a wave coming, and he jumps. And although he might dodge its impact, he's spending a lot of time being afraid of the next one. Because he knows it's coming. And as he's jumping and jumping, he's weakened each time. "How much more do

I have to endure? How many more obstacles do I have to get through?"

As The One, Marty can't appreciate all that he has done to care for Seth over these years, everything he has managed and made happen. He can't see the accomplishments. There's no time for that. He has to brace himself. He has to look out for the next wave.

PART III

No Good Moves

———

Work to deliver your bodies safely from
platform to platform, surface to surface.

Hold yourself; stand.

Stand and hold yourself while holding someone else.

Learn how the you of your body and me of mine
work our mutual instability together.

Learn how the instability of holding
while moving is a moment.

Learn that to move is to hold a we.

—PARK MCARTHUR AND CONSTANTINA ZAVITSANOS,
"OTHER FORMS OF CONVIVIALITY"

CHAPTER 11

Leaving It Behind

OVERFED GOLDFISH SLOSHED IN A GLASS SUN TEA JAR wedged between Tina's feet on the floorboard of the car. Over the last few months, her boyfriend, Ben, had forged ahead to Massachusetts for his first computer programming job out of college. Tina, a year behind him in school, had stayed back in Pennsylvania to graduate. She'd taken care of Ben's fish while he was away, and now they were huge.

It was 1995. Tina had finished her degree in applied psychology, with a focus on early childhood education. She minored in music. With college over, she was moving away from home and in with Ben. Shortly after graduation, they packed the car and made their way northward.

As Ben drove, she fretted over the fish, worrying they wouldn't make the trip. She turned over all this change in her mind. She was scared to leave where she had grown up and spent all her life; she was scared to leave everyone she knew behind. And she was nervous about her new apartment. She focused on the fish.

Mostly, Tina was nervous about what it would be like to live with Ben, because he was "normal." He had been the one who looked for a place for them to live while she was back in Pennsylvania. She told him to be sure to get a first-floor apartment, because she anticipated having trouble with stairs.

She realized there had been a miscommunication when Ben announced he had gotten them a basement-level one-bedroom in a large apartment complex. There were a few steps down to enter it. Though she was still able to walk then, she did have trouble balancing. As they drove toward their new shared life, those steps loomed; they were the first of many obstacles she was going to have to navigate.

———

Tina is a white woman who grew up in suburban Pennsylvania. At age six, she was diagnosed with a visual impairment that classified her as legally blind. In middle school, a state agency that worked with blind children regularly pulled her out of classes for sessions where she and other blind kids learned skills related to navigating the world as a blind person. Even though these other kids attended her school, she steered clear of them. She didn't want to be associated with them, she wanted to blend in with everybody else, she didn't want to be different.

Instead, she hung out with her siblings or other friends, kids who weren't disabled. She tried to be convincing enough to "get away with it"—to fool people into thinking she didn't have a disability. She wanted to be seen as not needing any help and did a pretty good job of seeming to be fine. But it took a lot of exhausting work on her part.

As a child, she struggled to imagine her future as an adult. She wanted to work, and she wanted to have children. But, she says, "I never thought I would get a husband." She didn't think she was desirable. She wasn't like her nondisabled sister, whom she thought of as beautiful. Instead, Tina was just blind. "I didn't think I had anything to offer anyone, so I thought I was going to be single. I thought I was going to be a spinster."

In high school, Tina's gait changed. She started to take double steps and began to lose her balance easily. She tried to ignore it and pressed on. After graduating, she lived at home and worked a variety of jobs—at a dry cleaner, a daycare, and babysitting. But a couple of months after her twenty-first birthday, she received a diagnosis of multiple sclerosis, or MS.

MS is a disease in which your immune system attacks your nerve fibers, disrupting your brain's communication with the rest of the body. It usually starts out with flare-ups that recede, which is called "relapsing-remitting" MS. Early on, Tina experienced symptoms like losing her balance or having difficulty moving, and then these symptoms would go away. But they'd always come back. Over time, it's common for relapsing-remitting MS to become permanent and degenerative, morphing into what's called secondary-progressive MS.

The diagnosis was traumatic for her. She already lived with her blindness, and now there was this. When her mom saw an ad in the local newspaper for an MS support group, she thought maybe it would be a good idea for Tina. Tina had lunch with a few people from the group, but once again, she wanted to steer clear. She focused on her other friends, the ones she went out clubbing with, friends who didn't have MS.

The following summer, Tina started to worry. *I've got to make more of my life*, she thought. She didn't want to live at home and babysit. She wanted to be independent and financially self-sufficient. She was especially afraid of "becoming dependent on any kind of [government] agencies."

Tina asked her mom about going to college. To her surprise, her mom said, "I was thinking I might go to college too. We could do this together." They shook hands on it and worked on getting her mom to be able to enroll, since she had never graduated high school. But because it had been so many years ago, her mom was able to get around that. It was official: They'd go to school together.

They enrolled in a nearby Penn State satellite campus. They drove twenty minutes or so to school together. Later, a professor suggested transferring to another college, a smaller one with old buildings and grassy knolls. Tina was a little nervous, but after both she and her mom got their acceptances, they enrolled once again and moved into a condo together.

She didn't stay in touch with her friends who had MS back home. She wanted to leave them—and the MS—behind. "I was doing something with my life. I didn't want to be pulled down with other people with MS. I wanted to wash my world of MS. I thought if I kept those friends, then maybe I would keep the MS too."

CHAPTER 12

The Tutor

AFTER GRADUATING FROM A VOCATIONAL HIGH SCHOOL IN Maryland, Ben had not been interested in going to college, but his parents told him he had to. It's not like he had another plan. He was kind of floating; he had a high school girlfriend and figured maybe he could find a way to make a life with her. With no ideas about where to go, he remembered he had seen at some point a brochure for a small school in Pennsylvania. The front of the pamphlet featured a picture of the campus, and one of the buildings looked like a castle. He applied to the school, along with a couple of others.

He got in and did well. He liked helping other students, and especially loved computers. He even assisted a professor in the computer lab sometimes. When students came in to use word processing programs, he helped them with technical difficulties.

The professor who ran the computer lab taught a computer class that Tina enrolled in, in her second year. Although Tina could see well enough to recognize people, she couldn't see well enough to read. One day, she was in the lab to take a test. Having another person be her reader was how she accessed exams.

Ben, a young white man with brown hair to his shoulders, was in the lab. "Could you read it to her?" the professor asked Ben.

"Sure," he answered.

Ben found Tina, who had curly blond hair and was wearing stylish jeans, at one of the computers. As he sidled up next to her and started reading the exam, he was very aware of how cute she was.

"She wasn't doing very well on the test," he laughed, "but I wasn't allowed to help her."

Tina enrolled in a psychology course the next semester, and when she needed a tutor, the person assigned to help her was once again Ben. Although he was a cognitive science major, he tutored lots of different subjects. Suddenly, they were spending an awful lot of time together. At first, they only talked about psychology. But they soon began to have long meandering conversations about other things, like their shared love of animals, and they got to be friends. And then, more than friends.

By the time they met, Ben had been in college for a bit. He was single and a "typical horny teenager," dating a few girls off and on. But Tina was different. She was "very attractive," but he also thought she was a ton of fun, which was Ben's main interest. She was always game to go out dancing, to hit the bars, and she told funny stories of growing up with her wild siblings.

From the start of their tutoring sessions, Tina loved his long brown hair and how confident he was. She liked that he was his own person. And she definitely didn't like it if she saw him talking with another girl in the hallway.

Ben noticed something was wrong with Tina's gait. When they walked together, she'd keep her hand on the wall or hold his hand to steady herself. But Ben loved how they could talk. They connected so easily. He began to feel like she was the right choice for a girlfriend.

Meanwhile, Tina worried about the MS and if he could accept her if he knew about it.

"I was truly scared," Tina says. "But I knew in my heart that honesty was the best policy, so I knew I had to tell him right away."

It was an overcast fall day when she did it. Gray and wet, with autumn leaves stuck to the cement sidewalk on campus, she got up and out for their scheduled tutoring session. As she sat down in a classroom with him, she was nervous and braced herself. He was sitting across from her, wearing his usual loose, stretched-out T-shirt and the jeans with a hole in the knee. So cute. *He's gonna look down on me*, she thought.

She laid it out for him.

"I don't even remember if he said, 'I know' or if he said, 'I was wondering.'"

And when I ask Ben about it, he doesn't remember either.

What he does remember is appreciating her toughness at pushing through such difficult circumstances. "When we first met, she was very active, and though she had the MS and it was affecting her, she still really enjoyed going out and doing things. Going to concerts, going dancing, all the usual things that college students like to do." He admired her ability to bounce back, to pick up where she left off after a flare-up.

Tina, however, mostly felt shame. She was ashamed of her gait problems, ashamed that her mobility was affected, and ashamed that her MS constrained what they could do together on dates. For one, she couldn't go to an amusement park and ride the rides, as the jostling and disorientation would make her balance and coordination worse. She was afraid to tell Ben a detail like this. Surely, she thought, this would mean that he wouldn't like her. Surely, he'd be repelled.

When she finally told him, he said he didn't like them either. Tina felt relief, but still focused on building a sense of commonality between them. Maybe, she thought, gathering up an arsenal of all that they had in common would protect her from eventual rejection.

As that fall semester slid into winter, final exams began, and stress levels rose. Tina went to the campus store and bought Ben a teddy bear. She wanted to give him a small motivational token, to let him know, *Hey, you can do it!*

They made plans to meet up that evening and go to the condo she shared with her mom. It was getting dark when he arrived, and it was icy out; an ice storm had hit the day before. They strode arm-in-arm to the condos.

On their way, they had to walk slightly downhill on part of the walk. Tina slipped and fell, kicking one of Ben's legs out from under him, causing him to fall too. She gathered herself, got back up with his help, and kept repeating how sorry she was. "It's okay," he said. But she was embarrassed. She was beyond embarrassed—she was devastated; she had been so excited to give him a present, to have a perfect evening.

This was, she tells me, the moment when she first began to think that maybe she could believe that he accepted her. "He put up with me. He put up with me when I tripped over my own two feet, and I pulled him down, and he made me feel okay about it."

It was as though he became her barometer; if he could accept her needs, then she could try to as well. But she had long ago internalized the idea that her disabilities made her a burden, made her undesirable. So how could Ben possibly love her?

Ableism isn't just embedded in our policies and systems; it is lodged within each of us, contaminating our ideas of what a disabled life can mean and corroding our sense of self-worth from the inside out. Tina was describing what disability scholars and advocates have termed internalized ableism. This refers to

the deep, penetrating shame that people can feel about their impairment. They may struggle with feelings of worthlessness, and
they may try to hide their disability and avoid others like them.
It affects each person differently, and intersects with other aspects of their lives, like race or gender. For Tina, it started when
she steered clear of other disabled people as a child. And it once
again snuck up on her as she began to date Ben.

On a broader political level, we use the rhetoric of dependence
to diminish people, so we can't be surprised when individuals
turn that dependency-as-disqualification logic onto themselves.
The specter of dependency, whether in the form of needing caregiving in intimate relationships or needing help from the state, is
something we use to hurt people and to make them feel lesser. So
Tina struggled to feel lovable. She feared that not being seen as
independent made her abhorrent.

It's not as though Tina worried over nothing. Dating while
disabled can be harrowing. Even now, decades later, disabled
people who try to date often experience others thinking that
disability is incompatible with sexuality, or that people with
disabilities should be avoided as potential romantic partners.

At the time, however, Ben just wasn't particularly concerned
about her disability. He had dated a woman with cerebral palsy
at one point. He didn't think MS seemed like that big a deal. He
doesn't remember being aware that it was a condition that would
get worse. He was aware only of how much he liked Tina and
how sympathetic he felt toward her when she would have these
relapses and be essentially paralyzed or need medical treatment
to manage a routine infection her body just couldn't handle and
have to be in the hospital. But she always came back. So, he
thought, everything should be fine.

After dating awhile, Ben invited her to Maryland to meet
his family. She thought, *Maybe this is for real? Maybe I am liked?*

Of course, after she returned to Pennsylvania she almost immediately landed in the hospital. With MS, the ups always came with the downs.

Tina tried to keep her reality inside, tucked away, as best she could. Her mom had always been her primary caregiver; she was The One who went to the doctor or the hospital with her during flare-ups, lived with her and made sure she was okay on the day-to-day. But the rest of the time, Tina went out with friends, forging ahead. She went to concerts, loved her boyfriend, and had a thriving social life. She was especially fond of dancing. "I was dancing, and dancing was keeping me strong. When I danced, I felt really, really good." It was her salve. "I did not impress Ben with my walking, but I was a pretty good dancer."

One night, after Ben had graduated and she was in her last year of college on her own, she went out dancing with a friend. It was a good night. She was having fun. She had a solid relationship with Ben. They were going to be together once she finished school. She heard the music pounding, she looked around the room, she soaked it all in.

Then something happened.

"Out of nowhere, I fell." The floor thudded underneath her. "I sat in the middle of the dance floor on my butt and shook my head no. I reached my hand up to my girlfriend to help me up." Three things went through Tina's head: She was utterly embarrassed and wondered if everyone was looking at her. She hoped she hadn't made the record skip because the DJ, who she thought was pretty cute, would kill her if she ruined his records. But mostly she was grateful Ben wasn't there to see it. It was a defining moment, a shift in her biography.

"It sort of hit me," she said. "Wow, maybe the MS is gonna win."

CHAPTER 13

In Sickness and in Health

BEN, TINA, AND THE FISH MADE IT TO MASSACHUSETTS. After moving into their new apartment and learning how to navigate the stairs carefully, they settled into daily life together.

While Ben worked, Tina stayed home. Even this early in her disease, with the unpredictability of it, working wasn't a possibility. She had worked at the daycare on campus during college, but she was often incapacitated by infections or other flare-ups when she might be unable to move or manage an infection. These flares would last for weeks at a time. It was worse by the time she moved in with Ben.

She worried about not being able to contribute to the household. "I would clean and scrub or organize, whatever I could do, or do laundry." She feared being unproductive, or that Ben would see her as a burden.

One day, she decided to clean the bathroom. "I really scrubbed at it and scrubbed at it so hard that I was staggering." When she got up, she walked through the house to the living room. "I was holding on to the table and the chair and the wall, everything, to get myself over to the couch." It was official, and it wasn't going away: "I was a wall-walker."

"Wall-walker" is a term Tina used to describe how she moved through space by using the built environment to hold herself up. Although she loathed having to do it, it was a tactic she used to avoid the thing that she was most afraid of—needing a wheelchair.

As the MS worsened, she responded by escalating her efforts to mask her needs. Every time she went to the bathroom, Tina leaned her hip against the counter. She turned so her butt was flat against it, supporting her. She unbuttoned and unzipped her jeans and then bounced a little, shimmying her pants down. Once she got them down, she mentally readied herself to hurl her body from the counter to the toilet.

She did it a million times, even though each time she did it she was terrified she wouldn't make it to the toilet, that she would throw her body and it wouldn't make the landing. Each time she thought, *What happens if I end up on the floor?* But it was the only way she could take care of toileting on her own.

Less than a year into living together in Massachusetts, Tina took the train down to visit her family in Pennsylvania for a few days. Before heading back home to Ben, she got dressed up. She was young and wanted to look beautiful. She put on a skirt, wanting to feel good about herself, to show up and have Ben see her as desirable, as worth missing when gone. "Hopefully, I presented myself to Ben like I was well taken care of, like I was ready to live a normal life." She clung to looking good and acting normal, even though when she walked, she sometimes had the sensation that she was falling, that the incline of the floor was telescoping toward her.

Ben picked her up at the train station and drove her home. She was tired, and together they flopped down on the bed. She rolled onto her side, propped up on her elbow. He looked at her like he was thinking hard.

"Penny for your thoughts?" she asked him.

"I'm not thinking anything," he said. But she was certain he was.

The next day, after a long day at the office, Ben came home to a sink full of dishes. The MS had gotten to Tina that day, and she couldn't wash them. Usually, she had a barstool at the sink to support her standing without falling to do it, but that day her balance was just too off. She was tired from traveling. Maybe it had been too much. She was sure she'd fall if she tried, even with the barstool there to steady her, so she decided to let them be, but she fretted.

When Ben came home, she told him it had not been a good day. She hadn't been able to do the dishes. She felt ashamed. He walked into the kitchen and started washing them.

Standing at the sink, he said, "Will you marry me?"

"Well, I probably would answer you if you asked me correctly," she joked. She was in shock. He took her comment to mean he should get down on one knee, so that's what he did. He dried off his hands and came to her.

Tina was stunned. "Here he was doing a task for me, and I had been worried he was going to throw it back at my face." She'd worried maybe he didn't think she did enough around the house. She was keenly aware that he worked, and paid the rent and everything else. She didn't feel like she deserved this, deserved him, deserved anything—but she said yes.

What Ben remembers most about this moment is the overwhelming feeling that she needed someone to take care of her and that he was The One who could do that better than anyone else. Marrying her would be an expression of that. He loved her and cared about her so deeply, and he also anticipated her deterioration. They were on their own now in Massachusetts. He had already taken over going to doctor's appointments and doing the day-to-day care her mom had once done. He assumed she would only live another ten years or so and he wanted to make them good ones.

By the time they moved out of that first apartment, Ben knew about that bathroom routine of hers. And it worried him. They had grab bars installed, but it still wasn't easy for her. She repeatedly broke the hinges on the toilet lid, and they'd have to replace them. Ben wasn't sure what else to do because she was determined not to ask for, or accept, his help. But the price of trying to pull things off on her own meant enduring a terrifying bathroom ritual multiple times a day.

In Tina's mind, needing help was such a shameful thing that she was willing to risk injury. "I had to show my independence," she said. She had so internalized that needing care was deplorable that she couldn't ask for it. Especially in the bathroom.

Her tactics didn't last. She got sick once and just couldn't manage it anymore. She was embarrassed to ask Ben for help, but it didn't feel like a big deal to him. He knew her body so intimately already. They'd been having sex for years, and though sex is a different kind of intimacy, he was unbothered.

"It's okay, it is what it is," Ben told her, and he got up and accompanied her into the bathroom, unbuttoned and unzipped her pants, pulled them down, and then pivoted her to the toilet. He didn't have any training for this. It was a process of trial and error learning to get her on the toilet safely while trying to avoid injuring himself, which wasn't always possible. She could still wipe herself, and so she did, then Ben helped her stand up and pulled up her pants. Ben accepted it in stride, but it didn't make her feel any better about it. She struggled to accept needing help toileting.

"I don't think anyone could have made me feel better because that's probably the lowest of the low," she says. "It was despicable."

And then there was the specter of the wheelchair. Her mobility issues were becoming untenable. She was still wall-walking, but it was hard. In moments of crisis when her legs would give out, Ben would drag her from room to room on a blanket, pulling her on it through the apartment to get her wherever she wanted to go. Something had to give.

LAZY!

"It's the first word that comes to mind, in big bold letters—I mean really big, like when you watch *Sesame Street* and you see a person and the letters are bigger than the person, that's what it felt like." All she could see was **LAZY! LAZY! LAZY!** flashing in her mind, in bold. But eventually there was no other choice. It was time.

Ben and Tina were married in October 1996. The day was perfect. The leaves were still mostly green, and there wasn't a cloud in the sky. It was a small wedding, with maybe fifty people in attendance. Folding chairs were arranged on a lawn with an aisle down the middle. Tina arrived from stage left, pulling up in a horse-drawn carriage to where Ben was standing in front of the guests.

Since Tina used the wheelchair pretty much full time by then, they decided to have her sit tall in the white carriage, wearing a white long-sleeved gown with an intricate bodice and plunging neckline. A delicate veil sat on her head, and white crinoline flowed behind her. Her blond hair was pinned in an updo, and she held a large bouquet of white tuberoses in her lap.

When the carriage came to a stop, Ben hopped up into it with her. He was wearing a black tux with a white bow tie and a white rose corsage pinned to his lapel. They took their vows together, including *in sickness and in health*.

CHAPTER 14

Around the Clock

As TINA'S MS WORSENED IN THE COMING YEARS, BEN slowly realized that his marriage to Tina would be the tool the state used to abandon her, and therefore him. He would be The One on whom the entire responsibility of her care would be consolidated—financially, practically, emotionally, physically.

"There's a common assumption the government will provide whatever services you need, which it doesn't," Ben told me.

Indeed, public perception is wildly different from reality. Not only do people assume millions are bilking the system for free SSDI checks (the disability con), but people also assume there are ample systems supplying long-term care. A 2019 survey revealed that "more than half (56%) of boomers mistakenly believe that Medicare will pay for their ongoing long-term care." It does not. While home health services from Medicare can be obtained in limited, specific circumstances, home healthcare (medically focused) is different from long-term home care (relating to activities of daily living or ADLs). For those whose disability doesn't come until late in life, aging in place is a pipe dream, unless someone volunteers to be The One to make it feasible. The public lie of the disability con isn't just ableist and wrong, it also forecloses productive conversations around shoring up long-term-care systems that people need at earlier ages as well as later in life.

Ben and Tina availed themselves of what support they could to help Tina get the care she needed. Namely, she was insured through Ben's work as a computer programmer, but she sometimes needed expensive treatments that weren't covered. Copays ate up a significant portion of their funds. They had to find housing that was affordable, but also wheelchair accessible. It was nearly impossible.

No matter how frugal they tried to be, living on Ben's salary and Tina's measly $400 SSDI check each month, which only covered groceries, became increasingly difficult. Her monthly check was much lower than someone like Ángel because she was so much younger than him when she was approved. The amount you receive is based on work credits that you accumulate over years of working. Qualifying so young, without much of a work history, meant her SSDI check was tiny. Plus, she needed paid help around the clock, but her SSDI was not enough to help pay for that either.

They began to do the only thing they could afford to do: Every morning before work, Ben set her up on the couch with all her needs within reach. He put the phone near her so she could call him if she got into trouble, and he would come home. Of course, Tina avoided calling. She felt like a real nuisance, so she tried everything she could not to have to.

Sometimes Ben had to leave a job because of the competing demands of being in the office and caring for Tina. "We'd have a crisis, and I'd have to take time off or work from home for a period of time." That didn't always go over well; his job was not always understanding. But there was no other choice when the MS struck and Tina was in a sick period. When she had an infection, which happened every so often, the interplay between the infection and the MS essentially paralyzed her.

Tina also periodically needed to undergo treatments that required a home IV; Ben needed to be home for those. Even though these treatments were often short-term, lasting a week or so, Ben struggled with balancing work and these care duties. Once, because his job was a twenty-minute drive away, he decided to work from home for the week. He sent a note to his coworkers each morning that he was working from home. "You can reach me on the phone. This is my number. You have my email."

Near the end of the week, his boss called. "Nobody knows how to find you. We don't know how to get in touch with you," he said. This didn't bode well. Back in the office a few days later, he was called into not just his boss's office, but his boss's boss's office.

"I know you've got a lot going on at home, but work has to come first. Work is most important, that's what pays your bills," the boss said. In his head, Ben thought, *No it's not. It's not the most important thing.*

He immediately started looking for a new job. There was no way he could care for Tina and keep this job if that was the company's approach. Just like millions of other caregivers across the country coping with a culture hostile to care needs and no system for home care, he tried to make strategic choices about where to work and how to meet Tina's care needs himself.

The Family Medical Leave Act (FMLA) went into effect in 1994—but no one ever told Ben about it. He wasn't aware this law existed. But it is also a limited provision. The FMLA allows certain types of employees (such as those working for an entity with more than fifty employees) to take up to twelve weeks of unpaid leave. Of course, Tina's disease was lifelong, not twelve weeks long, so this solved little.

Ben usually relied on vacation time or sick time to care for Tina when he couldn't leave her alone. It was exasperating. He couldn't afford not to work, but how was he going to work *and* care for Tina? How could he support them if he didn't work and cared for Tina full time? How could she have health insurance if he didn't work?

The conundrum Ben faced is wholly common. Nearly two-thirds of caregivers are employed, but research shows they struggle and must work less, losing $522 billion in wages every year because they must split their time providing care. For caregivers over fifty alone, that adds up to $3 trillion in lost wages, pensions, retirement funds, and other benefits.

So with no other choice, every morning, Ben set her up on that couch. Phone. Water. Food. TV remote. "Many times, if I ran out of water, I wouldn't call him. I would only say something after the fact," she told me. When he got home, she'd mention it and he'd leave her a bigger supply of water.

One winter morning, Tina was on the couch as usual. She had a blanket tucked around her, the phone and water nearby. Her lunch, a tuna fish sandwich, was made and sitting on the table next to the couch in a cold bag. Their two cats, Slinkey and Sunshine, were keeping her company.

It was just before noon. Tina was hungry and ready to eat, but she needed to go to the bathroom. She sat up and reached out to the wheelchair parked next to the couch, to transfer herself into it like she usually did. This time, she didn't make it.

She fell on the floor in such a way that her face was smashed down into the beige carpet. She couldn't move. Her head was stuck looking in one direction, toward the baseboard heater a few feet away. With her blindness, she stared at it and squinted, trying to make out shapes, discern light patterns. She was stuck in this position for the rest of the day.

Since she had tried to transfer into her chair to go to the bathroom, eventually she urinated. For the next several hours, she lay there on the carpet in her urine. At some point, she heard the cats. They must have smelled the tuna fish sandwich, because now they were after it. Somehow, they proceeded to get it out the bag and eat it, circling her, enjoying their meal while climbing on her. She was hungry, wet, and felt broken. She cried into the carpet.

Cell phones were not as common then. She couldn't move to reach the house phone and there were no neighbors to hear her. She thought about how at their next house, she was going to make sure they put in hardwood floors. She blamed the carpet for impeding her chair and causing the fall. *Never again*, she thought.

The winter afternoon wore on, eventually turning darker and darker, outside and in. As the sky began to shift into night around four, she tried to get herself up. She pushed. Nothing. She tried resting, saving up her strength for another big push. She tried again and again. Nothing.

As she lay there that winter afternoon, the main thought tumbling through her mind wasn't the lack of access to adequate home care in this country. Instead, she was thinking, *I never should have gotten married. Look at what I'm doing to Ben. He had a life that his family had envisioned for him and look at what I've done to it.*

CHAPTER 15

Couch Life

FOR THE NEXT FEW YEARS, TINA USED DIAPERS SO SHE would not have to transfer to her manual wheelchair to go to the bathroom anymore. The idea was not to have to get off the couch for anything the entire workday. She'd be safe this way, even if she had to sit in a soiled diaper.

Without home care, each change in her body required she give away more of her autonomy. Every progression of the disease became a matter of living at the edge of what was safe for her. And eventually, that meant couch life had to end. She could no longer be left alone.

They started paying out of pocket for a personal care attendant, or PCA. It was just for three hours a day, but with Tina's worsening condition the hours had to be increased over time. This ate up most of what was left of Ben's paycheck. They went deeper and deeper into debt.

In 2008, Ben and Tina gave up the house they lived in at the time and got their first mobile home. "We bought the mobile home using credit cards," Ben told me. "It amazes me that I still had high enough limits, but I used multiple cards to do it." That year, they also had to file for bankruptcy. He felt guilty about it, since it meant his debt just "went away," but doing so let them keep their mobile home, and the rent for the land it was on was manageable.

They spent a couple of thousand dollars making their mobile home accessible, like putting in a ramp. But they had experience with having to spend money on such things. In a previous home, they'd had to install central air because the MS made Tina's body extremely temperature sensitive. That alone cost over ten thousand dollars. Now they had to make renovations again. Everywhere they looked, they faced the extra costs of daily living that only disabled people have to contend with in an inaccessible world. Disability scholars refer to these added costs as the disability tax.

Struggling with housing and the costs of making it accessible is a good example of a disability tax. Most people don't know how difficult it can be to find an accessible place to live. Although the Fair Housing Act was amended in 1988 to prohibit disability discrimination, regulations intended to ensure accessibility in new residential construction pointedly did not apply to duplexes, triplexes, single-family homes, or mobile homes. Without a federal requirement to build accessible housing, developers and manufacturers did not go out of their way to keep disabled residents in mind. In a 2021 report, the Department of Housing and Urban Development reported that only about 5 percent of U.S. housing stock had accessibility features, even though approximately two in ten households include a family member with access needs like Tina's. It turns out, however, that those living in mobile homes are more likely to have accessible features like ramps than those living in single-family homes or apartment buildings. So a mobile home became their best option.

Meanwhile, Tina also needed full-time, round-the-clock care. The options were to continue to pay for a full-time PCA or home health aide out of pocket (they couldn't afford that), or they could pay for a PCA through private long-term-care insurance, but they didn't have that. Besides, Tina would never have qualified for it given her MS. Even though some people tout long-term-care insurance as a solution, fewer than one in thirty Americans have a private long-term-care policy to cover the kind Tina needed, and only about 7 percent of those over age fifty do. Such a piecemeal private market approach not only excludes people with conditions that warrant the care, purchasing LTC insurance also requires knowledge of financial planning and the resources to engage in it and obtain it as early as possible in life, or before you have a condition that would require care. All of this means that the most vulnerable and precarious among us are also the least likely to have access to long-term care.

The other option for long-term care is the one publicly funded program that provides home-care services: Medicaid. But this also wasn't an option for Ben and Tina. No matter what state you reside in, Medicaid has strict asset and income limits, requiring that you live in abject poverty to qualify. Medicaid is means-tested, and the eligibility limits are extremely low. States set eligibility limits in relation to the federal poverty level (FPL). In 2025, the FPL was $15,650 a year for an individual, and $21,150 a year for a family of two. People or families who earn even just a dollar more than these annual limits are disqualified. Under the ACA, many states raised their limits to 138 percent of the FPL, but this is still extremely low in terms of annual income.

In 2023, I spoke with Alison Barkoff, the acting administrator and assistant secretary for aging at the Administration for Community Living (ACL), an agency under the Department of Health and Human Services. The ACL has a mandate to fund aging and disability networks in every state to ensure that disabled people, including elderly people aging into impairments, have the services and supports they need to live in their communities. She told me that the biggest care issue in the United States right now is that our long-term-care system is primarily funded through Medicaid, a means-tested poverty program, rather than a basic universal resource. When a government agency's programs are means-tested, it spends time and resources determining eligibility rather than providing the actual services.

To address some of the gaps in our system, Barkoff explained, the ACL released the initial National Strategy to Support Family Caregivers in 2022. The goal of this strategy was to support unpaid caregivers like spouses and other family members. It also emphasized the interrelatedness of unpaid caregiving by families and the direct-care workforce crisis, with informal caregivers having to take on more and more.

In 2025, as I was finishing this book, the Trump administration announced it was eliminating the ACL. The ACL has given over $1 billion through grants to state and local governments, higher education, and small businesses to help do the work of supporting people who want to live at home, and to fill some of the gaps left by our lack of care infrastructure and sparse Medicaid supports. Now the entire agency is set to dissolve.

Each state also runs Medicaid differently. In Massachusetts, Ben's salary counted as income for Tina, disqualifying her. The FPL at the time when they really started to need round-the-clock care, in 2005, was $12,830 a year for a family of two. Ben's computer programming job paid him more than that, so Tina did not qualify, even though her ever-increasing care costs were eating up Ben's paychecks. For the next decade they pieced together as much care as they could afford with a few hours a day from a PCA out of pocket, but they were trapped, disqualified from state help, but too poor to afford the amount of care Tina needed.

Around 2014, Ben landed a job in Boston that changed everything. It was flexible; he could work at home when he needed. Over time, he went into the office less and less. It dawned on them: if he could work from home, it didn't matter where they lived.

"Let's go back and be closer to your family," Ben said to Tina. They sold their mobile home and later rented an apartment near Philadelphia. They chose an apartment that had an elevator and ample access to public transportation. It was way too small for both them and all of Tina's medical equipment, but the caregivers they could find didn't have cars and needed to take the bus or train. This location made that easy.

They still paid about $1,000 out of pocket for thirty hours of personal care a week. That was more than half of Ben's paycheck. "Thirty hours of care sounds like a lot, but when it's only six hours a day and you're taking care of the other eighteen, it's really not that much," Ben told me.

They continued to rack up debt, and bought groceries on credit cards. They had no savings. Something had to give. In Pennsylvania, they discovered Medicaid was a possibility. There, a spouse's income doesn't count against the applicant. It sounded promising, but it took more than two years of applying and being repeatedly rejected on the grounds that Ben's annual salary was too high; it appeared that the people working in the Medicaid offices didn't know the rules. He hired an advocacy organization to help him with the multi-office paperwork.

Eligibility rules for married couples are extraordinarily complex. I spoke with another spousal caregiver who lived in

New York State about this. His wife has a traumatic brain injury and needs twenty-four-hour care, but because his income and assets count against her, they too do not qualify for Medicaid. He was describing to me what is known as the "marriage penalty" for disabled people. That is, marriage equality has not been achieved for all groups in the United States because those who are disabled before marriage are often forced to remain unmarried, otherwise they lose their life-saving services and benefits. Similarly, those who become disabled after marriage don't get access to care systems such as Medicaid because they have a spouse who may have income and assets.

What I found in my conversations with people across the country is that we have expectations of love and marriage that are used as tools to siphon free care from a spousal caregiver. These expectations of romantic love are steeped in culture, but they are enforced through codifying strict eligibility rules for Medicaid that penalize disabled people for being married and ensure they are made to rely on their spouse. So this man in New York City with a wife who needs twenty-four-hour care was stuck, just like Ben. This man had income, but paying for care out of pocket was so expensive it was impossible. So his plan to get home care through Medicaid? Divorce. "It creates that kind of insane desperation between one thing or another. The choices are impossible," he told me. Divorce, he told me, is "for our future."

It was a surreal experience for him to show his wife the divorce papers and ask her to sign them, but she did. "You know this means nothing, right?" he told her. She told him she knew. "Then I said to her, 'You know I'm going to take care of you, right?' She knows."

Ironically, this man had to dissolve the social contract of his marriage—meant to guarantee a commitment between partners—in order to obtain the resources to secure home care for his wife.

This couple was engaging in what's known as a Medicaid divorce, which allocates all assets to the nondisabled spouse and avoids the couple having to "spend down" nearly all assets in order to qualify for services.

"This structure is completely broken. I have very strong feelings about it," Ben told me about his similar situation. But Pennsylvania was supposed to be different. Yet, "the people processing applications don't know what the rules are, various offices from county to state level don't talk to one another, and every state has different, complicated rules."

Over two years later, Tina was finally approved. "Getting approved for Medicaid was life-changing," Ben says. Tina was approved for care twenty-four hours a day, seven days a week. She was nursing home eligible, but Pennsylvania Medicaid supports home care. For the first time ever, they would have home care for Tina and not have to pay for it.

They are lucky that Pennsylvania supports home care. When we spoke, Alison Barkoff also flagged what's called the "institutional bias" in Medicaid. This refers to how federal rules require Medicaid in each state to pay for institutional care, but paying for home and community-based services (HCBS) is optional. About 90 percent of adults over fifty want to age in place, or stay living at home and in their community, but being left with no other choice but institutionalization is the more common outcome, even after qualifying for Medicaid. As such, repealing the institutional bias and advocating for the right to HCBS to be guaranteed in all states is "one of the biggest issues of our time," Barkoff stressed.

Since getting Medicaid, it has still not been easy for Ben and Tina. They've had to navigate learning how to use the benefit, how to get through all the bureaucratic hoops; they've had to figure out the best number of hours and shifts and become bosses of a sort to the people who end up taking on the job of home aide. The aides often don't show. They are not paid directly by the state, but by private companies who are contracted by the state to provide the services. These companies pay so little that it is difficult to find people to reliably do the work. Indeed, home health aide jobs are some of the lowest-paid jobs that exist, and have one of the highest turnover rates. In 2022, the turnover rate for the industry was nearly 77 percent. Yet the Bureau of Labor Statistics predicts the demand for home health aides will make it one of the top twenty fastest-growing occupations in the United States over the next decade.

These labor conditions, such as poor pay, that aides must work under emerge directly out of overtly codified racism: When the New Deal was enacted in 1933, domestic and farm workers were specifically excluded from labor protections, and by an interesting coincidence, these were jobs that were disproportionately filled by people of color. The category "domestic worker" is what home health aides belong to today. This workforce is primarily made up of women of color and those New Deal labor protection exclusions still apply.

———

Of the forty-four couples I spoke with across the United States, only five of the disabled spouses had Medicaid. Of those, only three had access to home care. While not all state Medicaid programs have home care, some of those that do have a provision for what's called consumer-directed care at home. "Consumer-directed" means that the Medicaid beneficiary (the "consumer") can interview and hire people to be their PCA, rather than go through an agency. This allows people to choose their own caregivers.

Some states even allow you to pay your spouse as your caregiver. For this to happen, the disabled spouse is assessed and a number of hours determined—say they are given twenty-five hours per week—and then, if their state allows it, their spouse's salary for caregiving those twenty-five hours is determined based on an average of the wage for an aide in that state or region.

One of the people I talked to about this was sixty-six-year-old Donna in Arizona. "It's a lot of work," she tells me, describing how she was able to get approved for this program. Donna found out about this possibility when she was at the beauty shop one day. She was talking casually about caring for her husband when one of the women working there told her how she has a friend who gets paid for taking care of her husband, and that Donna should investigate.

Donna was shocked, but also skeptical. "Anything I've ever tried to get for him, it was like 'No, you make too much money. No this, no, no, no.'" But she decided to explore it. "I checked out the long-term care, all that paperwork, oh my god. You would not believe the hell they put you through. Copies of taxes, and this and this, or why did you do this? What's this money for? Ay-ay-ay."

Frankly, Donna thought it would be a waste of time. But to her surprise, the State of Arizona said she was approved and sent a caseworker to her house. He assessed her husband and determined how many hours a week he should get. Then he gave her a list of agencies to choose from, and that's who pays her. Once again, because we have opted to create markets out of caregiving, she does not receive money directly from the state; rather the payment she receives for her care labor is contracted out through private agencies.

The caseworker checks in every ninety days and, generally,

Donna says, "It's a very good idea, and it does make me feel a little bit better, I feel I have a job. This is a job."

In California, one man I spoke with gets paid to care for his wife through the state's In-Home Supportive Services program (IHSS), which is available only to Medicaid (called Medi-Cal in California) recipients. "I came home on Friday the thirteenth of May, 2016, and I found her on the kitchen floor," he explained. They were both in their forties at the time, and this day became the new axis upon which their entire world would now spin.

His wife spent over a year in rehab. While there, staff told him about the IHSS program for paying a family caregiver such as a spouse, and they did all the paperwork with him. He had to undergo training and onboarding, but it worked. He felt capable and prepared once she came home. Until then, he had been working as a car driver, but the possibility of being paid to care for his wife made quitting to become her caregiver seem like the right call. Plus, he gets to be with the love of his life, which is what he wants more than anything.

CHAPTER 16

To Move Is to Hold a We

PENN GREEN MOBILE HOME PARK SITS OFF A SMALL TWO-lane road about a mile from a large cloverleaf interchange on the Pennsylvania Turnpike. Between the highway exit and the entrance to Penn Green is a series of industrial businesses. Cranes and bulky construction equipment line chain-link fences on the edges of gravel lots; small used-car dealerships advertise their wares.

The mobile home park is well manicured, with one-way streets so narrow they barely fit one car. On a Monday morning in August 2021, I wound my way through them to Ben and Tina's second mobile home, which they'd purchased in 2020. It is white with gray shutters, and at the very edge of the park, faces east over a small green field.

Inside, it was quiet except for the Westminster chime of the wooden pendulum wall clock over the mantel. Every fifteen minutes, the clock rang. At the top of the hour, it played the melody and then chimed the number of times corresponding to the hour. It was chiming nine times now, but Tina's home health aide, Mary, still hadn't arrived. Like every weekday, she was supposed to be in at six.

In Tina's large bedroom, Ben moved swiftly around her. He had gotten Tina out of bed and into her motorized wheelchair. She was wearing a white T-shirt and a pair of disposable underwear. Ben slid the arm of a cozy plaid flannel shirt up her left arm, then expertly leaned her torso a bit forward to pull the shirt across her back, sliding the right sleeve over her arm and up, then adjusting it. It was on and sorted in a matter of seconds. Then he grabbed a folded white bedsheet and laid it gently over her bare legs. He retrieved the hairbrush from the dresser across from the bed and brushed her hair.

"Ponytail," she told Ben.

"Got it."

Her aide not showing meant Ben had to split duties between caregiving and his paid job, and that Tina wouldn't get to do much today, like bake a cake or fix dinner, things she usually did by directing Mary. She has become adept over the years at telling aides how to execute tasks, using their body as an extension of her own.

One of their cats entered the room meowing as Ben put the hairbrush back, and then, already knowing what Tina wanted to do next, he reached above to a small shelf mounted on the wall. He moved his hand slowly across it, surveying some perfume bottles, waiting for Tina to tell him which one to grab.

"CK One," Tina said.

"Got it."

He wordlessly sprayed a little on her shirt and put it back. Anticipating her next need, he walked over to the bathroom adjoining her bedroom, wet a washcloth, and squeezed it out.

When he came back in, Ben put it in her right hand, which was lying on the wheelchair armrest. With some effort and concentration, she brought it to her face. To do this, she very slowly bent her neck to bring her head down and a little to her right.

Once she got the washcloth to her face, she swept it in slow motion across her forehead.

The only movement that Tina has left, aside from occasionally being able to wiggle a toe, is a little in her right hand and forearm, and her head and neck. Although her right arm is technically still functional, she has poor coordination. She can drive her electric wheelchair using the rubberized joystick, and most of the time she can use a cup with a straw and not spill it. But her coordination problems make these small movements fatiguing. Her balance is also not great, so she can't sit unsupported. She has a neck rest attached to her wheelchair that helps, and it's ideal for her to have something to lean against on the side, like a small pillow.

"I feel pretty good," she said about all this. "I'm grateful that I can still do some things right now."

She lowered the washcloth to wipe her cheeks, swiveling her neck slightly to the left and right as she held it there.

"Wait," she said, as Ben took the washcloth after she finished. "Do my ears." Ben wiped in and around her ears with the cloth.

"Thank you."

"You're welcome. Want to come out and get some breakfast?"

"Very much."

Ben headed toward the kitchen and Tina turned her wheelchair toward the door using the joystick on the right arm of her chair. The door had an extra-wide frame, but she was just a bit close and the side of the chair rubbed along the door jamb. The friction made a slow squeaking noise.

"You're supposed to stop when you hit things!" Ben said from the other room.

"It was only the—" She didn't finish the sentence because they've had this same exchange hundreds of times. Her visual impairment meant she was sometimes slightly off the mark getting around.

She headed slowly down the widened hallway, through the living room, and to the kitchen. They had spent tens of thousands of dollars again redoing this mobile home, just as they had the last one.

As I walked behind Tina, I saw a framed photograph of the two of them on the wall near the kitchen. It was a professional picture, taken right after college, and they were looking somewhere off to the right of the camera, Ben sporting a wide, easy smile, and Tina looking delighted. Her lips were curled upward, and her nose crinkled, as though she were giggling. In contrast to his shorn hair now, in the picture Ben had the long brown hair of his youth sweeping down his forehead and shoulders, while Tina's hair had that signature look of the time: high, puffed bangs, a perm. They were frozen in time. Now, Tina rolled down the ramp and past the photo while the clock chimed its melody again.

"What do you want for breakfast?" Ben asked Tina while standing in front of the kitchen sink.

"Cream of Wheat."

Ben crisscrossed the linoleum-tiled kitchen preparing her food. Tina's iPhone rang. Ben stopped and hit the answer button, set it to speakerphone, and put it in Tina's right hand. "Hello?" she said. This all happened wordlessly and instantly. He had already returned to making breakfast when his phone rang too.

While Tina made arrangements with her doctor's office for a follow-up appointment, Ben handled a work call. When they were both done, they talked about their shared calendar and Ben got her new appointment logged on it.

"Do you want anything in this?" Ben said, gesturing to her bowl.

Tina decided on honey and butter. His phone chimed again. It was Mary. She explained over text that she was very ill. She slept right through her alarm. She couldn't come.

Ben and Tina immediately decided it was not worth it to call the home health agency and try to get a backup person. They usually weren't successful anyway, and if they were, it would be many hours later. Better to just muddle through with Ben splitting his duties. Plus, I was there.

"I can be an extra pair of hands," I said. "I've done this before."

Ben nodded.

"Am I feeding you or just putting the pillow on your lap?" Ben asked.

Tina used the wheelchair controls on the armrest to recline her chair a little and asked for the pillow. Ben put it on her lap and nestled the bowl on it. This was an ingenious way to shift the starting point, situating the bowl higher, at the top of her belly, and closing some of the distance that her hand and forearm were going to have to travel.

She worked methodically. She concentrated, slowly scooping Cream of Wheat onto the spoon. She brought her hand up toward her mouth and leaned her neck down and to the right to meet her hand. While she slowly brought up the spoon, she stuck her tongue out on the approach. It reached out from her mouth to meet the bite of food piled onto the spoon, to help it along, to bring it all the way in, like a frog snatching a fly, but in slow motion.

"My back is kind of hurting from the chair. It's digging in my back, below my shoulder," Tina told Ben. Ben immediately got a pad from another room and slid it between her upper back and the chair.

"Much better. Thank you."

"You're welcome."

A moment later, Tina used her hand to slightly shift the bowl toward Ben. It was the smallest movement, the tiniest gesture toward him.

"You want me to do the rest?" he asked, in response to her barely perceptible signal.

She nodded. "Scrape the bowl."

Ben scraped the food strewn across the bowl into a pile, the metal spoon clanged on the ceramic, and he casually fed her the last couple of bites.

"Thank you."

"You're welcome."

After she had her final bite, Ben washed the bowl as he took a breath and looked out the window, over the pothos plant—also known as the devil's ivy—climbing along the windowsill.

———

Ben and Tina's interactions were a stunningly fluid intimacy of synced movements and strategies. If disability is that space between what our bodies can do and what the world thinks they *should* be able to do, Ben and Tina lived there with an enormous amount of creativity and competence. It was not just fueled by Ben's expertise; it was Tina's too. Over the years, she had learned to ask for what she needed, and their collaboration helped achieve it. The two of them had what disability justice activist, writer, and educator Mia Mingus called access intimacy. "Anyone can experience access intimacy," she wrote. "Access intimacy is that elusive, hard to describe feeling when someone else 'gets' your access needs. The kind of eerie comfort that your disabled self feels with someone. . . . It can happen with complete strangers, disabled or not, or sometimes it can be built over years."

While their routines were so honed, so elegant as to seem almost easy, underneath the smooth surface of their interplay—of the intimacy they've built together over decades of coordination—was something far more complex, a sadness. Because this dance, as beautiful as it was, was also a product of years of cruelty from an ableist world that had left the couple alone without any other resources but each other. For each of them, the *I* had been forcibly absorbed, taken over by their singular, partnered *we*. In the absence of collective care on a larger scale, there had been no other option, there had not been a greater *we*.

Even now, with Medicaid, Ben could not leave his house for more than a few hours at a time. Maybe, if a good aide that they trusted was there, he could get out for the day. But the truth of the matter was that Medicaid home care was the couple's only other source of help outside their relationship, it was help they'd waited decades for, and because of the constant undermining of Medicaid and its funding, this help was not always reliable. In 2024, Ben told me they only averaged eight hours a day, two days a week of aide care, though they qualified for twenty-four hours a day, seven days a week. With the wages for aides being abysmal, it would always be hard to find enough people up for the job. "I'm probably going to be doing this into my nineties," he told me.

Despite moving nearer to Tina's family, they still felt very much alone. Tina's mother had died when Ben and Tina were still living in Massachusetts. Other members of her family visited sometimes, but Ben told me, "They don't want to do any hands-on care, which is disappointing."

Without a collective support system and robust home-care

services, Tina's pathway to a good life was entirely consolidated onto Ben. The pressure on them both was enormous. If
Ben wasn't willing to be or could no longer be The One, Tina
would end up in an institution where the likelihood of neglect
would be much higher. Neither of them wanted this nightmare
scenario.

There had been talk of divorce about five years into their
marriage, around 2001. One morning, Ben walked into the bedroom, put his hand on Tina's foot, and said, "I want a divorce."
Tina froze. She couldn't say anything.

Ben brought up divorce because of the way the disease
was changing both of their lives and their relationship. They
went to marriage counseling together to try to work things out.
After a few sessions, it didn't seem to be helping. Instead, it
seemed to make things worse. They had more arguments after
sessions and nothing resolved, so they stopped going to therapy
entirely.

They carried on. And they maintained a sex life up through
2016, when they were living in Pennsylvania. Ben told me the
sex was quite good in college and in the first few years of their
marriage, but that over time, as Tina became more disabled,
physical intimacy became harder for them. It was a lot of work
for him to set it up, position her, then clean up afterward. A
major turning point for Ben came because of a C. diff infection Tina had around that time. C. diff can be iatrogenic,
an infection that patients in hospitals can get and that causes
inflammation in the colon. "After changing diarrhea-filled
diapers repeatedly, I just didn't see her in that way anymore,"
he told me. This was a final straw for Ben; he simply shut the
sexual part of himself down.

When I asked Tina about the loss of their sex life, she told
me she suspected that Ben had always thought of her as "inept

at sexual relationships." As her disease progressed, she felt that Ben no longer saw her as capable of sex, though she disagreed with this assessment.

"He is so mistaken," she told me, and she was hurt. "I struggle to feel desirable," she said. When I asked her if she would be interested in sex if he was, she told me yes, but that "he has cut the line." Then she added coyly, "But god works in mysterious ways." We laughed. "And you can use that quote!"

Almost twenty-five years later, in 2025, Ben still wanted a divorce, but chose "not to act on it." When I asked Tina how this affected their day-to-day life, she answered, "Tension. A lot of tension." They continued to be together and share a life, but it was extremely hard. She tried to stay positive, to make things more cheerful, but it was difficult. Most of all, she was embarrassed to tell people about this, to talk about divorce. "I feel like I'm a failure . . . that I don't know how to make another person happy."

The result was that Tina must live in the knowledge that Ben is not happy, but also that her survival depends on his willingness to stay. This is why when the aide doesn't show up or there are no aides to work a shift, it makes everything worse. When what little moments of caregiving help they get are taken away, their relationship is stressed. Ben's burned out and deeply upset by it, while Tina is furious "because somebody is playing with my marriage." She sees what it does to Ben, which makes her feel worse. "It makes me very angry and tense and I want to kick and scream," she tells me.

Meanwhile, Ben realizes how horrible divorcing her, or wanting to divorce her, sounds. Early in their marriage, he and Tina went to an MS camp for adults. A lot of people there were single, Ben said, because their spouses had left them. "I thought it was so sad. How could people do that? I understand now." But

Ben is so stressed from being abandoned by our society to meet all of Tina's care demands that he finds it hard to be a whole person with a self-determined life. He has lost thirty pounds in the last few years. But while he might experience far less of this kind of stress if they were to get divorced, he could not bear the thought that Tina would be exponentially worse off.

Indeed, these were the exact reasons why Tina, from the start, refused to entertain even the idea of divorce. She knew that everything for her would collapse: housing, food, her personal care. "Everything gets affected by it," she told me when we chatted in 2025. She must perpetually confront the concrete limitations of her body, while also knowing that her quality of life entirely hinges on Ben's willingness to be there. In the face of state abandonment, she holds the memories of an untold number of hours of her life that were reduced to sheer survival and bears witness to Ben's struggle to carry all the responsibility. They've both ended up being slowly destroyed by it.

For the most part, the divorce question just looms, seeping into their everyday life, knitting together tension across their interactions, even as their relationship is so intimate. Usually, they did not talk about it directly. But every four months or so, the divorce question pokes its head up. "It seems to be something we bring up when we want to hurt each other," Ben told me. In Tina's view, she thinks Ben wants to be free of her. So when she's mad she'll say, "Boy, you really want that divorce, don't you?" And when he's exasperated, he'll say, "I think I'd be better off alone." And then they carry on, day by day, year by year, trapped in a position where neither of them have any good moves to make.

———

After breakfast, Tina needed to go to the bathroom. Ben walked out of the kitchen to prepare. Tina turned to me and said wistfully, sincerely, "I'm so lucky. I'm so lucky to have Ben." I heard the gravity in this statement. I heard it in the thank-yous she repeatedly uttered; Ben was her lifeline. What if he were to take it away?

Her thank-yous were a courtesy, she said when I ask her why she kept saying it. They were meant to show Ben her appreciation, because she worried he might think she didn't recognize all he does. So she said thank you again and again. "I'm not even thinking, it just comes out. If I don't say thank you, I feel like this heavy weight is on my shoulders, like I've done something really bad. I can't really explain it."

Tina headed into the living room while Ben walked over to the Hoyer lift that's parked next to the commode. The days when Tina could hide her toileting needs were long gone. Now, the whole set-up was right there in the living room.

Ben stepped on a small lever to release the brake of the lift to wheel it over to her. It was basically a tall metal pole, about Ben's height, sitting on a large, wheeled, U-shaped base. The legs of the U extended about three and a half feet. At the top of the pole was another metal arm that stuck out horizontally, parallel to the base. A T-shaped bar hung loosely from the end of this, with metal loops on each side so one can clip the ends of a sling onto it.

The Hoyer lift was invented by a quadriplegic man in the 1940s. Ted Hoyer, who had a spinal cord injury as a result of a car accident as a teenager, regularly needed to be moved from his wheelchair to his bed or elsewhere. With no way to do so, he spent years tinkering and eventually, in collaboration with his cousin, designed and built a device that would become the Hoyer lift. The cousins even did repairs and modifications on wheelchairs for other disabled people. Like Ángel and his hacks, the Hoyer lift is an example of the ingenuity of disabled people.

Ben unlocked the brake, swirled the lift around easily on the laminate floor, and pointed the legs toward Tina. He steered the main shaft of the lift, which had metal handles on either side of it for him to hold on to, closer to her and locked the brake again. Moving Tina from the wheelchair or recliner to the commode, which had a curtain rod and curtain around it for privacy, was a huge part of daily life. Multiple times a day, they used the lift to move her more easily.

Ben expertly slid a U-shaped sling under Tina. Once she was in and he clipped the sling onto the loops on the lift, he pressed the lift button. The arm of the lift raised as the motor, which ran on a battery, hummed. She was then suspended in the air, her lower half naked so she can urinate or have a bowel movement once she was lowered onto the commode, a very tall PVC pipe chair originally intended for showers, which had lockable wheels, a padded seat, and armrests. They've slid a five-gallon paint bucket with a thick black trash bag in it under it. He closed the curtains around the commode. While she sat, Ben and I chatted casually about their cat. Tina urinated.

"I think I can get up," she said, after a few moments.

He walked behind the curtain to the commode and opened a package of wipes. He dropped down on one knee and reached underneath to wipe her.

"Thank you," she said.

"You're welcome."

He took the bucket away and the sound of the lift began again.

For many, the idea of dealing with another person's urine or feces is abject. But these are natural bodily functions that we all experience, and a disabled body needing this kind of help embraces this essential truth of being alive. Disabled people have the profound expertise of figuring out their bodily needs and working collaboratively with caregivers to get them met, and in the process, they acquire powerful knowledge that could help others move toward love and acceptance of their own bodies. Still, how many times have you heard someone say casually, "If you have to help me with *that*, just put me out of my misery"? This is yet another normalization of an ableist way of thinking. While having to be helped with toileting is often held up as a loss of dignity, there is no shame in tending to our bodies. This was simply how Tina did things. This was her body now, and it is a worthy one. She has become so used to it over the years that while she was in the lift, she casually made her grocery list. Midair, she called out to Alexa to set a reminder to pick up cereal.

Besides, from such needs came the legacy and utility of the Hoyer lift, which cannot be overstated. Seven decades later, Ted Hoyer's design still dominates the lift market. In 2024, the "patient lifting equipment" market was set to reach $5.4 billion, an increase of more than $2 billion since 2019. It's not just Tina and Ben who rely on a lift like this; so do millions of others. Care needs around toileting are common and they are valid.

"It's not a big deal anymore," Ben said. "Yes, there was a period of time it was upsetting for her." But over time, they both got used to it. It got better. It got easier.

"It's just a regular occurrence around here," Tina told me with aplomb.

When I think back to my time helping J or working as a

direct-care provider with disabled adults when I was in college, I think about all the disabled people who have shown me how to accept the fact that we all need to urinate and defecate. These needs just are; they are what we all have to do as humans. Our disgust and denigration of needing help with toileting is more harmful than the need itself. When we frame people's needs or realities as disgusting, we are not only suggesting that disabled people are less than and unworthy of that care, we are also recoiling at these natural processes in ourselves. In truth, we are lucky to have those who can teach us how to learn to live with these universal needs.

Ben rolled the lift across the floor and over to the sitting area near the front window. Two recliners looked out onto the open field, trees swaying in the wind. After getting Tina situated into hers, Ben went back to his office to work.

A few moments later, Tina told me that her feet needed to be elevated. She used the remote on her recliner to elevate the footrest and asked me to put a pillow under her legs, to keep her heels from touching the footrest. It was important to do this so she didn't get pressure sores.

I picked up one of the pillows and tried to slide it under her legs, which were surprisingly heavy. I felt like I didn't know what I was doing, or what the best technique was. Then she asked for a light blanket and instructed me on which one to get.

"Want me to fold it this way?" I asked, holding it up.

"No, the other."

I turned it, and eventually she said it was fine, and I laid it down over her. I suspected it was not fine, and she was just being kind.

After a while, Ben emerged from the office, and without a word he corrected the pillow and blanket, moving seamlessly. I thought to myself how obvious his technique was once I'd seen it. He made it look so easy. *Why hadn't I thought of that?* I wondered.

While the clock on the wall chimed noon and played its melody again, Ben made sandwiches. Still in her recliner and looking out the window at the grass and the trees and the perfect blue sky, Tina said this new mobile home was better than all the other places they'd lived. She liked the view, and the fact that an occasional group of deer would pass through on their way somewhere else.

Ben brought over her lunch and set it on the pillow that he placed in her lap. He took a seat in a wooden chair near her and scooted it over, close to her elevated feet. He balanced his plate on the tops of his knees and ate his sandwich with one hand. They both looked straight ahead, in silence, at a world in motion on the other side of the glass. He put his other hand on her shin. It was a loving act, subtle and unprompted.

PART IV

Can't Contain

Compassion, stretched to its limits,
is going numb.
—SUSAN SONTAG, *REGARDING THE PAIN OF OTHERS*

CHAPTER 17

Fix It

THERE WAS A TIME WHEN JADE THOUGHT, *WE CAN HANDLE this.*

She first met John over the phone. It was 1990, and she worked for a California nursing agency, where she processed payroll. At the time, Jade was twenty-six years old with a BA in accounting, having immigrated from the Philippines. She had come to the United States on her own, leaving her family behind.

John, a thirty-nine-year-old white man who worked for the agency as a licensed vocational nurse, or LVN, had found a mistake in his pay and called to complain. Jade told him to bring his paper time slips to the office so they could go over them. He came in, she helped him, and that was that.

Then, a day or two after their meeting, he called the office again and asked her if she was married. He had noticed the ring on her finger. It was her mom's wedding band; she wore it to feel close to her faraway family, a special reminder of them. She wasn't interested in dating, so she lied. "Yes, I'm married and I have three children," she told him.

To help his case, John activated what he called "the Filipino Connection," referring to the high number of Filipina nurses in California, where more than 20 percent of nurses are Filipina. This statistic is explained in part by the global care chain phenomenon, a term used to describe the migration of people, predominantly women, from poorer countries to countries like the United States, where there is a care crisis. More and more women migrate to other countries to meet the ever-increasing demands for paid care work in eldercare, childcare, disability care, and nursing that our lack of social safety nets creates.

Having learned from the other nurses that Jade had lied, John decided he'd just have to be persistent. He called every day, and he had a colleague put in a good word for him. Three months later, they went to dinner. "I was attracted to him and he was interesting to talk to," Jade told me. Six months later they were engaged, and a year later they were married.

They were a happy couple. John was an attentive and loving partner, a romantic who frequently bought Jade flowers and jewelry. "He really treated me like a princess," Jade told me. And they just got along. He was caring and helpful; she didn't have immediate family nearby, and he taught her about American culture and was supportive of her as she later shifted into a nursing career. "We were good—we had a good sex life, good communication, he cared about the things that mattered to me. . . . We had a lot of maturity in the relationship." There weren't a lot of fights; if she was upset about something, she'd go quiet until she was calm and they could figure it out. When he was upset, John, who loved running and did it often, would go for a run and then return when he was ready to talk. They made a good home, a good life, and they had three beautiful daughters to show for it.

But then, John began coming home from runs with scraped-up knees. He started to inexplicably fall, lose his balance, or trip. His handwriting was changing, becoming smaller and smaller. In 2000, he learned he had Parkinson's disease, a movement disorder located in the nervous system, that worsens over time. In its later stages, it causes a decline in cognitive function in addition to the physical losses. John was forty-nine years old at the time of his diagnosis, Jade just thirty-six, and the girls two, six, and eight.

By then, Jade had finished nursing school and was working as a registered nurse. So when John was first diagnosed, Jade's immediate instinct was to learn everything about Parkinson's and then use her training to battle it. She was motivated to approach their situation intellectually, professionally. But of course, caring for her husband was nothing like helping a patient she might see in the clinic. "This is no ordinary patient," she told me.

In nursing school, she learned about common signs of a disease like Parkinson's, like tremors or a shuffling gait. But she wasn't given information in her training about the emotional and psychological effects on the patient and the family. John would have delusions, obsessive thinking, and overwhelming impulses to gamble or shop. No one had told her about this aspect of Parkinson's, and she ended up learning about it from reading caregiver blogs or talking with other caregivers for people with Parkinson's.

About seven years after John's diagnosis, his father showed up one day on their front porch, with luggage. Until the day that he died in their house eight years later, Jade performed the bulk of her father-in-law's care too. John helped some at first since his disease was in its earlier stages then, but like millions of other women in the United States, Jade was The One meeting the multigenerational care needs of aging parents, an ill spouse, and her young children, with very few social safety nets or immediate family nearby to support her. In fact, she routinely sent money back to the Philippines.

Jade's can-do attitude propelled her through the chaos of the coming years. But after her father-in-law died, John declined rapidly. Jade was left alone to take on all the household respon-sibilities: She had to work to pay the bills and take care of the children at home. She learned to survive on four hours of sleep, but she could never keep up. "You're trying to go up to the sur-face of the water, and then something just pulls you down," she told me on one of our phone calls. The first time we spoke, we did so over video; her computer's camera was high up on the desk so I was peering down at her. It felt easier and more intimate to switch to phone calls after that, her voice calm and measured each time we spoke.

Career-wise, she was held back from increasing her earning potential because of all the caregiving demands. She was unable to ascend the proverbial professional ladder because she needed to be home as much as possible. She couldn't attend industry conferences or take advantage of other opportunities for profes-sional advancement. Instead, she was picking up more and more nursing shifts just to pay for the family's expenses, while doing the caregiving for John herself.

At home, she didn't feel she could be there for the chil-dren as much as she wanted to, or as much as they thought she should. It felt impossible to keep up; something always seemed to be slipping through the cracks. And when it did, she was aware that it appeared to everyone to be her own failure. "Mom is an easy target for everything that goes wrong," she tells me. Once, Jade was at a conference across the country. John, who was still ambulatory but experiencing some cognitive con-fusion, was at home. He wandered off and the police had to come find him.

For a while, she switched to telephonic nursing jobs so she could both work and provide John's round-the-clock care at home, tending to him between calls. Her work was deeply im-portant to her. She wanted to be good at nursing and advance within it, but instead, her job became something she just had to check off the list. Because of the caregiving, "I'm just meeting the minimum, just so I don't lose the job."

Eventually, she sold their house to pay for John's care. She took a more stable job that required her to go in for her shifts. Since John couldn't be left alone anymore, she used the money from the house and her better job to pay for his care out of pocket while she was at work or with the kids.

The losses accumulated; the years passed. She began to expect chaos, to expect that her care work would never be finished. "You'd fix one thing, and it was like, oh my God, here is this other issue—his incontinence. What can I do so that the pee will not seep through the sheets for the next three hours? But all I have to do is change the pads . . . you figure out a way to do it. Then, a week later, something will change, and you have to figure out a way again. . . . Over the years, I have learned that there's no permanent fix. You just fix it."

As more and more, and then everything, eventually fell to her, she looked around and asked, "Where did my life go?" The material losses of her home and her career dreams, along with the depression, the loneliness, and the sheer burnout and grief of watching her husband deteriorate was killing her. By 2017, nearly two decades in, emotions began to push their way up; the can-do attitude that had fueled her for so long was simply running out. She could no longer push through by ignoring her feelings.

She and the children, much more grown by then, went to family counseling. She found a support group and learned about the Well Spouse Association. She saw that they were having a national conference for spousal caregivers, a whole weekend of events that provided the opportunity for spousal caregivers to connect with one another and form friendships, and also to hear research and education on caregiving issues. When I asked her how she found the WSA, she said she discovered it online in the middle of the night.

I could just picture it; I had been there too. Lying in the dark, searching the screen while J slept in the other room—that's exactly how I found WSA as well. Surely, I had thought, there was some answer out there to all my pain. Surely, it was just a matter of me looking hard enough to find the thing that will ease it. You begin to think of the pain you carry as another problem you are supposed to solve, another task to take care of, because everything around you tells you that you're supposed to be able to handle it. So you try to make the pain just go away; that way you can keep doing it all.

Jade attended that spousal caregiver conference. In a large conference room with maybe a hundred other people, the speaker asked the attendees to turn to the person on their right and say something they've always wanted to say but never felt they could. Jade turned and looked her neighbor right in the eye and said, "I am so angry."

CHAPTER 18

A Good Wife

FEELING ANGRY, MUCH LESS SAYING IT OUT LOUD, WAS completely out of character for Jade. She never would have admitted it to anyone before, let alone herself. But that day, in the safe environment of the WSA conference, among other spousal caregivers who could understand what she was going through, it hit her all at once—the exhaustion, the grief, and yes, the *anger* of having become a serial caregiver.

When the session was over, she went back to her hotel room and cried. She could not stop crying. She tried, but her body simply wouldn't stop. She spent the weekend sobbing, her body rolling with unbridled emotion. "I was really brought down to my knees," she told me. The depth of her anguish astonished her.

When Jade and I first spoke in 2020, it had been twenty years since John's diagnosis, but only a couple of years since that pivotal weekend of the WSA conference. By the time we talked, John was receiving hospice care at home. His condition fluctuated: some days he was bedridden and in clear decline, then he would have an upswing, and was eating better, gaining weight, and even ambulatory with assistance. So not only was she carrying the past—decades of emotional fallout and exhaustion—but she also couldn't be sure which trajectory he was on in the present. Should she be bracing herself for his imminent death or would he be stable for a while? She held all the possibilities at once, suspended in uncertainty. And she knew there was no emotional relief in sight, no matter which way things went.

Between our conversations during this time, she sent me a photo of her and John. It was a close-up of them sitting together on his hospital bed, their cheeks smashed together, both smiling. I was struck by their love, the purity of it, but also by all the ambivalent and conflicting feelings I knew she was having. I wanted to know more about that weekend, the turning point in her emotional landscape. "Tell me more," I said.

"That was really the first time I realized I was angry. Because I'm a good—no, my image is this: I'm a nurse, I will take care. I'm a good wife, I can't be angry, I have to be understanding."

A good wife.

I felt her words, her aspirations, her desire to be good in my bones. Because I too had been desperate for that nice, neat narrative, where my capacity to love and care for J remained bottomless. I had wanted not only to care for J, but to be happy doing it. I thought I could somehow acquire integrity through sacrificing myself. So I understood Jade's impulse, her framework for understanding her position, and recognized myself in it: To bear it all is to be "good."

In my conversations with Jade and so many others I spoke with, and from what I knew from my own caregiving with J, it was clear that there was a right thing, an expectation, threaded through all our experiences. With no real care infrastructure to help families, the care vacuum is filled with a slow and steady hum of powerful messages about who should take on this care instead (mostly women), and how you should feel about it.

The state doesn't just abandon disabled and ill people by deeming them not worth committing public resources to. State abandonment is also achieved by the successful coercion of family members to take on the material care the state refuses to provide. Caregivers I spoke to had internalized this, acquiescing to the belief that it was their own individual duty.

Enter the idea of the self-sufficient nuclear family, in particular the dream of monogamous coupledom and the fantasy of a spouse, usually a wife, who can be endlessly mined as a fount of free love and care. The message is this: If you are a good spouse, you should be able to endure. You should be able to fill this void because it is your duty. It's right there in your vows: *in sickness and in health.*

So many people I interviewed believed their role was to do all the material labor of their spouse's care. But it was also true that there happened to be no other option. "I'm just adhering to those vows. If I had a choice, I wouldn't be doing this," one person told me. Others said the vows meant they must stay and complete the job, do the work. Still others said things like, "I was raised that marriage is a commitment, it's a lifetime thing."

While any family caregiver faces the pressures of being The One in a society with few safety nets, spouses are particularly vulnerable because of our beliefs in the primacy of the romantic couple and the presence of legal vows. I found that this was borne out in caregiving research too. Compared to other types of family caregivers, such as adult children caring for their aging parents, research shows that spousal caregivers have far more intensive care demands that they carry out almost entirely alone. They do more medical and nursing-level care—almost three-quarters report doing so while a little over half of other caregivers do—and are more deeply involved in monitoring conditions and managing medical care. They do all this caregiving almost entirely alone, and while feeling that there is no other choice.

I spoke with the psychologist, consultant, and caregiving expert Dr. Barry Jacobs about the research I'd found and what

I was hearing in my conversations with spousal caregivers. He told me that marriage vows are a key reason why spouses are expected to take on the primary caregiver role. Over his many years of seeing patients who were seeking therapy and support as caregivers, he has concluded, "For spousal caregivers it's like, 'You signed up for this. These are part of your wedding vows. This is your duty.'"

It's as though we believe the extent of what someone is capable of as a caregiver is magically transformed by the mere existence of the words *in sickness and in health*. But it is an utter fantasy to believe that a spouse's love alone gives them the capacity to carry the weight of an entire social system's abandonment without dire consequences for everyone involved. But this fantasy is precisely what makes the cycle of abandonment complete, because as the state shrinks away, we as caregivers are told that if we don't take it all on, we forfeit our ability to be "good." And so, we try and we try and we try. And in that trying, we often abandon ourselves.

———

A good wife.

The "wife" part is especially important because care is so deeply gendered. Men become caregivers too—I spoke with many of them—but more women than men are caregivers, likely because patriarchy socializes them to do that work and women have historically been relied upon to provide that care. The scholar Jina B. Kim describes this idealized version of the role of women and femmes in families as "the Wife," who essentially functions as a "needs-fulfilling machine" so that any kind of collective or state-level care can be abandoned.

In Jade's idea of a "good wife," it's clear that she understood her value as a person, her goodness, to be contingent on her extreme willingness to care. This idea that it is a woman's role to do care work is so entrenched, so normalized, that women who are thrust into caregiving roles often do it to an extent that is detrimental to themselves. Aside from not having choices or other resources from which to get help, women are often taught it's simply what we are supposed to do. The data also bear this out; men leave their sick wives more often than the reverse.

I was technically not a wife to J, but a femme partner. Women are so socialized to be caregivers that in lesbian worlds, it is a common phenomenon for them to become immediately enmeshed with their romantic partners. There is even a classic lesbian joke about it: What does a lesbian bring to the second date? A U-Haul.

I am also an eldest daughter. Raised in a context where my mother went absent, I was a teenager when I became The One who packed the lunches, bought the groceries, and scrubbed the stains. So with J, I rose up to meet the familiar ghosts of my childhood; my skill sets had already been mapped onto me by a culture that sees the domestic sphere and the work of care primarily as women's work.

Care responsibilities fall especially hard onto women of color, whose communities experience higher rates of disability and illness due to structural inequalities. All the while, they are even more socialized to and expected to carry it all. And for immigrant women, particularly Filipina women like Jade, there is a long history of migration and transnational experiences that are shaped by their gendered understandings of what it means to be a wife, mother, and also breadwinner.

Jade was no exception. Marriage means you do not leave, she told me, especially when someone becomes ill. She described her beliefs as coming from her Filipino family, how important family commitment and caregiving is to her and to all the people in her family, especially the women. Her mother would turn over in her grave if she left her husband, she told me. And her daughters? She wanted to model for them what marriage looks like. And to Jade, that meant demonstrating that marriage means you stay no matter what.

She tried as hard as she could to stay afloat, to push against the tide that just seemed to keep rising. But slowly she realized that being "good" was coming at the price of her mental health, her sense of self, and her emotional safety. She was drowning in levels of sadness, exhaustion, and anger that she didn't even know she was capable of feeling. She couldn't see a way out.

I heard this description of emotional breakdown again and again from caregivers, and even experienced it myself. We revere the romantic couple in our culture, yet use it as a site of extreme extraction of care labor with no regard for the mental health effects it may have on the caregiving spouse. Research shows that those in more intensive caregiving roles, such as spouses, have "the greatest slides in self-rated health." One-third of spousal caregivers report their health has worsened, compared to just 21 percent of other family caregivers. These declines for caregivers in intensive caregiving roles aren't just physical: alongside physical pain, the majority report depression.

———

After the conference, Jade found a way to cope with the emotional fallout that would let her swim, or at least not drown. It was a way she could contort herself to somehow meet all the demands, to keep going despite being decimated from the inside out.

She made this choice because she knew there was just no room for her feelings to get in the way of what needed doing for John's care. Breaking under the strain would be a failure. So she found a way that would let her have some respite now and again, some relief, while still holding on. But it broke all the other rules of being a "good wife," and so she had to keep it secret.

CHAPTER 19

No Saint

SOMEWHERE IN THE DECADES OF JOHN'S ILLNESS WAS THE slow disappearance of who she and John once were as people, what they once were as a couple. This included the evaporation of their romantic and sexual relationship. In the beginning, Jade hadn't realized just how much would slip away and how alone she would feel, how much it would hurt. "You deal with it," she told me, "until you can't."

"I never had a problem with the physical care," she told me. "But the emotional . . . He's always going to be my husband, but the dynamic of being a romantic object and lover to a caregiver . . ." She trailed off.

Jade worked hard to adjust her expectations over the years. She tried to adapt to the changes in their dynamic. She wanted to reimagine what a romantic partnership could be, given these new constraints. She wanted to find a way to be The One who handled all his care—and to stay in love with him at the same time. She knew that the "good" and right thing to do would be to accept what was happening and not feel dissatisfied in her relationship. But it felt impossible to do that amid so many profound losses.

The things John used to do for her as a partner and lover gave her great joy. She held on to memories of the flowers he used to bring her, the sweet, tender moments they had, the date nights, the physical intimacy they had shared. But as the years wore on, there was no more relating in those ways. So much had been taken away from them.

There was no more sex; it was no longer a possibility. Nor, later, did John have the cognitive capacity to understand that these losses were happening between them. Jade was desperately grieving their love and sex life, but the one person in the world she wanted to share her grief with was no longer available. With his failing cognition, it felt to her like the man she married no longer existed.

The deep pain of losing sex and romance came up in many of my conversations with spousal caregivers. For many ill spouses, sex just wasn't physically or cognitively possible, and most caregivers did not want to have sex with their spouses anymore.

This pattern of decreased sexual desire in the context of spousal caregiving is borne out in research and can be summed up as "when care goes up, sex goes down." Studies consistently show that regardless of the type of impairment an ill or disabled spouse has, the more assistance they begin to require, the more the caregiver's perception of the relationship shifts. Caregivers often describe no longer feeling that their role is a sexual or romantic one; instead they report experiencing themselves as taking on a parent-like role. This is an enormous loss. After all, sex is typically the very thing that sets a romantic relationship apart from most other relationships.

The overwhelming majority of caregivers I spoke to responded to questions about sex with a resounding *no*: "it's off the table," "gone," "zero." I was not surprised to hear these answers to my questions. J and I experienced this loss too.

After the initial months of our whirlwind romance, we never had sex again, not after her bone marrow transplant, nor in the years that followed. Part of it was the physical decimation of her body. Part of it was the worry and terror I was constantly experiencing. Another part was that something had fundamentally been altered between us.

I often felt strapped in, forced to watch J slowly wither away, one horror after another, without relief. Even in periods when she was ostensibly doing "well," it never felt safe to relax. So many things had gone wrong that we were constantly bracing for the next disaster. It was lonely, terrifying, and required constant anticipatory grief to stay ahead of all the losses.

Abstractly, I felt sexual desire, or at least wanted to. But actually making sex happen between us often felt incongruous with the situation at hand. Besides, J was having her own difficult relationship with her body, coping with her own grief and trauma. She was abruptly put into menopause because of the treatments for her cancer, and she never felt good. She found it difficult to imagine being the kind of lover she once was: confident, mischievous, attentive. She mourned the loss of this part of herself, as did I.

One night in 2008, two whirlwind years after J's bone marrow transplant, I woke in the middle of the night and it finally hit me: I was in a sexless relationship.

I slipped out of our bedroom while J slept and wrote in my journal that my body felt dead, that I felt desperate for J to touch me, to reach out and grab me with some feeling of desire. *I haven't felt it in . . . years*, I wrote. *I feel sick to my stomach at this statement.*

A fundamental sense of myself as a young person, as a lover, as a partner, had slipped away. I didn't want it to be gone. I wanted, more than anything, simple, pleasurable sex, like she and I used to have. I didn't know if either of us could do it again; any physical intimacy at this point would be so fraught with grief, laden with the emotions of everything we had endured.

After years of never being touched, I began to shut down that part of myself. I found the most solace in the memoir *Dirty Details* by Marion Cohen. She said that it wasn't just her spouse's progressive disease that was chronic, so was her grief. "Chronic grief can feel scary," she writes. "Detached. Unreal." To protect yourself, you have to separate in a way, "unbond."

My grief told me to constantly prepare myself for the next worse thing. J's disease felt simultaneously like a never-ending and an ever-imminent death spiral. In this context, what happens for spousal caregivers is a kind of letting go of your partner while still intensely caregiving and performing all other typical duties of a spouse or partner. The incongruence, the complexities can be imperceptible to those on the outside, but internally it becomes a high-wire act, a dual track that spousal caregivers must operate from. We learn to compartmentalize in order to live with the deep pain of our status as spouse and the conflicting realities of daily emotional life.

To make things worse, we have to keep it to ourselves. "Our grieving seems to violate various rules," Cohen writes in her book. That is why I felt the need to hide my grief. The slow detachment it caused *did* break the social expectations of spouses to maintain romantic love no matter what, but reading that book I learned that the struggle wasn't unique to me. When I looked into the research on maintaining a romantic relationship as a caregiver after hearing struggles on this front from others in the research for this book, I found that there are data showing that the declining mental health of the caregiver—demolished after so many long-term demands and the trauma of having to watch a partner suffer—negatively affects their capacity to engage in a romantic relationship.

So, it did not surprise me that many of the people I spoke with had completely disengaged from the possibility not just of having a sexual relationship with their spouse, but of being a sexual person at all. It was a loss, but it had to be buried deep inside to be endured. Letting that part of the relationship completely wither away and disappear can sometimes end up being the least painful choice.

Studies show that younger caregiving spouses experience these changes even more painfully and profoundly than older caregivers. Younger caregivers question their role and identity because they may experience incongruence between how they had envisioned their role and what it turned out to be. Thus, they feel they must either change their identity or try to intervene in some way. To achieve congruence, some alter their expectations, some engage in other coping mechanisms, like dating and having affairs. This topic is profoundly understudied, a taboo topic that researchers haven't spent much time on, even though it is a regular occurrence.

I was glad that people were willing to talk to me about sex and intimacy. I hoped that it gave them comfort. I too struggled with the loss of a sex life with J. I was ashamed. I was young—how could I accept this? And I knew that my disabled friends would likely be horrified by the suggestion that a disabled person's partner could no longer feel sexually interested in them. It felt like I was bad for feeling that way.

There are ableist myths that disabled people aren't sexual beings or that disabled people should be infantilized. I didn't want to take part in that. But I also had to reconcile how some of the caregivers I spoke to described feeling like they were in a more parent-like role with their spouse. I felt that way sometimes too. J had some cognitive issues, so I had to explain things over and over, and as the illness progressed I sometimes didn't know if she'd be coherent. How do you make sense of those kinds of feelings while caring for a spouse, someone you're ostensibly supposed to view sexually? There was no map for this.

To be sure, not all spousal caregivers lose their sex life. There are huge differences in the experience of caring for a sick and dying person, or someone with cognitive decline, versus being partnered with someone with a static or stable disability, and everything in between. Many disabled and chronically ill people are quite capable of having romantic and sexual relationships. Some caregivers I talked to still had sex with their partner, although their number was few.

In his book *Disability Theory*, disability scholar Tobin Siebers argued that we don't often think about sex alongside disability. Yet, doing so, he said, "broadens the definition of sexual behavior" and "reveals unacknowledged assumptions about the ability to have sex." When I think about being expansive with ideas of sex and intimacy, I think about a woman in upstate New York who told me how she could crawl into her husband's hospital bed and snuggle with him. It was a revelation!

I think about Denise in Massachusetts, with her partner, Sara. On the one hand, she told me, "The basic loving and caring about each other is still there," but then she paused, fighting back tears. She had to gather herself; the loss of their sex life was a source of profound grief for her. "It hasn't really been anywhere close to sex-type stuff in a long time." But when she does PT exercises with Sara, Denise will sweetly hold her hand. This means something to them.

Sometimes it's a matter of dealing with the loss of sensation, or a catheter, maybe it's balance issues and falling down in the middle of sex. From my experiences in disability communities, I know that sometimes it's simply about figuring out a better position. Disability cultural knowledge teaches me that bodies are hard to live in and we just have to work with them anyway. And when you move forward without ableism, everything can be negotiated.

While every situation is different, it remains true that ableism is a sneaky thing haunting all aspects of our lives, and it lurks even in our most intimate spaces. It produces the limiting belief that disabled people can't have sex, don't have sex, aren't desirable, or must have bad sex. It's important to refute that ableism, even as most of the stories I tell are precisely about the loss of sex when you're a caregiver in the context of illness.

———

Despite all the losses, Jade tried her best to reimagine their shared world, but as she did, John slowly drifted into his own separate one. Things shifted. Their romantic connection and sex life were no longer, but in their place came something different. A different kind of love. It was no less powerful, but it was different.

She continued to care for him, but the loneliness grew in Jade's core, spreading and blooming across every part of her. Nothing eased it. She thought that maybe friends could fill the emotional and romantic void, but she did not have time to nurture many friendships. Plus, people were uneasy around illness. Friends stopped visiting or calling. They didn't know what to say. Dozens of other caregivers I had spoken to told me the same thing: Friends disappeared, their world got smaller, everyone seemed to want to forget about them, to look away.

When people ask Jade how she manages, "I never know how to answer that question," she told me. "I'm no saint."

The next time we spoke, Jade called me from a parking lot. She had a few minutes to spare and so she curled up in the front seat and called. After a long pause and with confession in her voice, she ventured to say, "Laura, I have to tell you something."

I heard her shift uncomfortably in her seat.

"It's not something that I share with just anyone. I think it's appropriate for this setting, so you have a complete picture of me as a caregiver. It's important that you know."

I had a sense of what was coming.

"I'm trying to get enough courage to tell you this," she says. Pause.

At that conference for caregivers she'd attended, the one where she sobbed for days, a man gave her his number. He did not live near her, but as a caregiver too, he understood her pain. They started talking on the phone over a course of months. They eventually met; they had sex. They saw each other only a few times since he lived far away. "It felt so good to have that," she said, to know he was thinking of her, that she was desired.

Her affair was rejuvenating. It had been years since she cared about what she looked like. It had been years since she dressed up. And for him, she wanted to. It was glorious. It gave her energy to get through, to keep caring for John.

It's not like she hadn't tried to be okay with her loneliness. Over the years, she bought herself flowers like John used to do. She bought a journal, took herself down to the ocean to look at the view. She watched the sunset, writing down her thoughts, trying to practice a deep kind of acceptance of her fate.

But when she really looked inside herself, she didn't want to take in a sunset by herself or go out to eat for a nice meal alone. Some people can do this, she knows, but it had just been so many years—decades. The loneliness was destroying her from the inside out. She didn't want to feel dissatisfied, but she couldn't help that she did not want to be alone anymore. She wanted to share these things with someone, but she also desperately wanted to be a good wife and take care of John.

She can't tell people she had an affair, she told me. She knows they will never be able to understand. "Other people have relationships outside of their marriage and people will still be forgiving," she says, but the calculus is different for spousal caregivers. "For us, they're not as forgiving, because how can you do that with your husband so sick?" Plus, she said, if people found out about the affair, it would erase everything, all those years of caregiving would simply be negated. "It's only: How can you do that to your spouse who is so helpless and needs you?"

So Jade knew that no matter how "good" she had been, no matter how much caregiving she had done all those years and was still willing to continue to do, the minute you cheat, you're no longer a good wife. If people were to find out the desperate ways she was contorting herself to try to survive in a role that was hollowing her out, she knew it would mean forfeiting being good, even as she continued caring for him.

But none of this is to say that Jade was interested in playing the victim. She was not. She knew that what she latched on to to stay afloat, what she had needed to carry on, was viewed as unacceptable. But she had made her choice. So she kept it a secret and asked me in a whisper, "Am I a bad person?"

CHAPTER 20

The Gray

JADE WASN'T THE ONLY CAREGIVER WHO TOLD ME ABOUT having had an affair.

Forty-year-old Yvette became a caregiver for her husband, Tom, after he had an anoxic brain injury. Suddenly, he needed round-the-clock care at home, including help with all his activities of daily living, his feeding tube, and many medications. Unlike Jade and John's situation, it was not a slow decline. When Tom's brain injury happened, "Everything shattered in an instant, it wasn't a slow loss of hopes and dreams that we had. It was just—everything was gone."

Like Jade, Yvette told me that she started out in "full caregiving mode." But to do so, she had to cordon off who he was to her in her mind. "He was initially just the patient because I couldn't have him be both a partner or spouse and grieve that and care for him. There was not enough capacity in me."

Yvette and I talked on the phone for the first time in 2020, seven years after Tom's brain injury in 2013. She told me, "I feel a lot of pressure to still act like a perfect nuclear family. I am supposed to be the committed wife who was going to take care of him."

It's not that she doesn't want to care for him. Yvette takes the expectations of family seriously. She grew up in a very religious Chinese American family, which has shaped her sense of moral duty. "That part has been tough because there is this moral layer attached to what my friends and people who love me believe for themselves. I think they're much more black-and-white. . . . But the world I'm living in is not black-and-white."

About a year before our conversation, Yvette decided to start dating. Her husband had full-time home care by then, things had settled a bit. She was a thirtysomething with young children. His disability was not progressive; he would need the same level of care for the rest of his life, and Yvette wanted it to be a long one. She began to envision how her life would unfold under these circumstances. She told a few friends she wanted to date. Some were supportive, others uncomfortable.

Unlike other caregivers I spoke with, Yvette talked to her husband about it. "I initially wanted him to understand, and I wanted him to agree and to give consent to it. I wanted it to be ethical because that was really, really important to me . . . not anything that felt like betrayal. I didn't want to lie, I didn't want to hide, but I also don't want to cause him more pain."

She decided to start dating partly because she became acutely depressed. "I was just suffering, and I felt like I needed connection. And I had reached out to him for that connection, and he did not respond."

He was understandably upset by her desire to date, she told me, but he eventually acquiesced. They came to an agreement: "He could ask me anything and I would be honest, but I would not volunteer any information. That felt like the most protective of him and his feelings."

After a few years of dating, she eventually met someone, fell in love, and started a serious relationship. On a phone call in 2024, Yvette told me about him. His name was Brian.

It was a difficult process to share her relationship with Tom, but he slowly began to accept it. As Yvette and Brian's relationship continued, Brian came to dinner, joining the children and Tom at the dinner table.

But in 2023, Tom passed away. What she is most grateful for is that Tom got to meet Brian. It comforted her to know that Tom knew the person who would be in her life, and in his children's lives, moving forward. Being with Brian and having him meet Tom meant there was continuity in her family story. It's unconventional but it felt more connected.

"It isn't necessarily a happy ending," Yvette stressed to me. Tom is gone. This was an enormous loss for her, and for their children. On the one hand, the approach she took gave her permission to unfold into her new self in new, beautiful ways while Tom was still alive. She told me it gave her a chance to "re-find the parts of myself as a woman and a person that I had lost in the intense caregiving."

But on the other hand, she still grieves for Tom. She grieves for the life she had originally dreamed of and lost. Brian is wonderful, but this is not a do-over, she tells me. There are no do-overs. While having a new partner helps in the wake of Tom's death, it doesn't fix all that she has lost. She doesn't want anyone to think that because Tom is gone and Brian is there that she is okay.

"I am not okay," she told me.

———

What struck me about other stories of infidelity was how for some people, having an affair seemed to be the answer to surviving their role as The One without sacrificing their mental health entirely. While some spouses let their sexual selves die in response to the end of their romantic relationship with their spouse, for others, survival required finding their sexual or romantic selves elsewhere.

There was the man who was a caregiver for his wife with a brain injury she acquired when they were both in their thirties. "How can you have sex with a person who in the middle of it says, 'What day is it?' She was not connecting in any way and so I backed away from that." Thirty years later, now in their sixties, they are still married, but there is no romantic or sexual relationship. "I am not in love with her . . . but I do love her," he told me.

His values, informed by his religious beliefs, are intricately linked with the vows he took. "I'm still married, and my vows said that when I'm married I keep my zipper up. But I still owe it to myself to have friendship." Having romantic friendships is his way of trying to reconcile his values and his vows.

Then there was the man who had affairs, both before and after divorcing his wife, who had a brain injury. For decades he has been deeply involved in caring for her, sharing a home, and arranging for aides to care for her. But the reactions to his affairs were different depending on his marital status. Prior to the divorce, if people found out he was dating, they thought he was a bad person. Once the divorce went through, however, people would say, "Oh they're not even married anymore, and he still cares for her?!" He was now a saint. "Just hearing that you're not married changes the whole paradigm," he told me. "'That's a good man! What a nice guy!' people would say."

A woman in her forties told me that her husband was twenty-five years into his progressive disease and now qualified for hospice. In her thirties, there was a period when she felt like she was slowly breaking. She was anxious and depressed all the time, and because it was happening to her at a younger age, her peers couldn't understand, and she felt profoundly alone. "I was no longer functional," she told me.

Her husband wasn't just physically declining but also cognitively. The physical care demands she could manage, but she couldn't bear the loss of the mental and emotional connection because of cognitive changes. "The cognitive stuff is not great," she told me. "He's a different person than he was. I wouldn't have married this person."

A few years ago, she met another spousal caregiver with whom she started having an affair. Because he was also a caregiver, she felt he could understand; they were part of a special kind of a family, she said. It was important to her that it be kept in the caregiver world where the complexities of her life would be understood. She did not think it was something she could share with other people.

"The secret no one talks about," she told me, "is that having an affair is the one thing that can bring you back to life." Having an affair reminded her she was a whole person, outside of caregiving. It revealed all the parts of herself she had shut down. She felt both joy and pain in rediscovering them because, under the circumstances, just knowing those parts still existed would have to be enough. "My values won't let me leave," she told me. As for her vows, "I felt I had to break one of them to have the strength to uphold the others."

The experience of having an affair changed her entire outlook on the world. "Before, I could live in these black-and-white extremes—good people do this and bad people do that. But I live in the gray now." Her affair is over, but she feels it is important to talk about it because sometimes in the context of spousal caregiving, the relationship itself is just not good anymore. "With spousal caregivers, there's no room for a bad relationship when you're at this stage," she explains. Because they are ill, even if it has decimated their personality and their cognition, "People just expect you to stay, even if everyone else in the world would get to leave."

————

In a culture that has divested from our collective care and has declined to take on a shared responsibility of care in our communities, having a sense of individual goodness amid it all can feel like The One's only currency. We praise caregivers as "saints" and "angels," but these platitudes often only serve as a lure so that we will continue to accept things just as they are. But social and political arrangements based on neglect, based on a lack of public care infrastructure, create a violent context for caregiving, for caregivers and care recipients alike. Because the idea that caregivers are saints directly links to the stereotyping of disabled or ill people as burdens and charity cases. To continue withholding public resources, the state first casts disabled and ill people as adding no inherent value, as burdens to society. Valorizing caregivers with empty platitudes but no real caregiving help, therefore, functions as a tool to justify state abandonment.

Despite providing this care, and often doing so in extreme circumstances without any other help while coping in complicated ways that are fraught with ambivalence, in our culture, caregivers are often flattened into a caricature. They are seen either as *good*, because they're these angels willing to do it all and forfeit their own wholeness in the process, or *bad*, because they can't function like that. I think back to Jade talking about wanting to be a "good wife," which essentially meant to forfeit her own needs, while silently breaking apart inside. I think back to the many stories of struggling spousal caregivers who turned to extramarital affairs for relief. I think back to myself during my years as a caregiver, desperately wanting to be "good" within these systems, and always feeling like I was failing.

Jade likely asked me if I thought she was a bad person because she knows what the broader culture is saying. We've all seen the scandalous headlines: "Woman Divorces Her Husband While He Was Dying of Cancer." "The Ultimate Betrayal: I Cheated on My Dying Wife." "Cheating on a Sick Spouse." The comments sections of these articles are full of moral outrage: marriage vows mean nothing these days, sacrificing yourself is the ultimate way to show love, people are so selfish, cheating is a sin, integrity means not breaking your vows, a caregiver's pain is nothing compared to the spouse's experience of illness.

But behind the scandalous headlines are the dark, murky spaces in which people are trying to live. Everyone I spoke with very much took their vows seriously and were practically destroying themselves to keep them, providing care with little to no help. Others took great pride in adhering to their vows, referring to them as the very reason why they stayed, and why they felt motivated to continue caring for their spouse.

But the bigger picture is this: We simultaneously place the monogamous couple at the head of a nuclear family and deem this the only acceptable arrangement, while putting people in the impossible position of doing it all. We do this to get away with not investing in disabled and ill people's care as a matter of our collective human welfare. This is a delusion of individualism and individualistic ideas of care; you cannot consolidate all the care onto a spouse without undermining their capacity to be one.

The reality is that the fantasy we have of the couple cannot contain the intensity of all the demands of life, of these fallible bodies we must exist in, when we must do so without care infrastructure. So when I think about the people who told me about their affairs and how they chose to "live in the gray," I feel sympathy, affinity even. I see how they were trying desperately to feel fully human within their dehumanizing circumstances. And I could understand their impulses because I had done that too.

In the earlier years after J's transplant, I had turned the romantic and sexual parts of myself off. But eventually, as more years passed, it started to become unbearable. When I decided to explore my desires again, it wasn't necessarily about wanting to have a sexual self. It had more to do with the fact that I had begun to descend into a mental health crisis, into a distorted, horrifying fun-house version of myself. While trying to keep up with the demands, with the pressure to carry on, alongside the further and further decline of J's health, all the while my mind was splitting apart. Something had to give. So when caregivers told me about their affairs, I did not judge them. I felt for them. I know from experience that you have to be in extreme pain to make that choice.

———

John died in 2022, about five years after Jade went to her first spousal caregiver conference and twenty-two years after his initial diagnosis. She still has a relationship with the man she met at the conference.

It was never about the sex, she tells me, it was the connection—him saying good morning and good night, the stream of texts to let her know she is not alone, that she is seen. "You've changed a diaper one hundred times today and you have lifted him and your body's aching and you can't tell the children . . . and there's the person you can run to."

As John slipped further and further away from her, Jade realized, "You need a witness to your life and nobody can do that if not that partner, because nobody else knows you like they do. . . . I didn't realize how important it was to have that person. It's always nice when you know someone in this whole wide world is thinking of you that way."

Since John's death, she has continued to wrestle with it all, sparring with her own values, with being raised Catholic, with what her mother, if she was still alive, might have thought. But she's more comfortable now; she's at peace, she's forgiven herself. She has told her daughters. She has tried to make sense of it all. Still, she carries the grief of the life she lost, the years she held on, the love she had for John and all that they both endured.

Now, Jade helps others by running support groups for spousal caregivers. By the time they find their way to the group and to her, most of them have been "brought down to their knees," she said, like she once had been. She's the one picking them up now, she tells me. This work gives her a sense of purpose, of meaning. She went through so much without help, but she knows they don't have to be alone anymore.

CHAPTER 21

Not Well at All

As Jade ran support groups for caregivers trying to survive the mental health effects of their experiences, I was hearing more and more difficult stories of other caregivers across the country. Particularly, the story of sixty-six-year-old Lily in Maryland, who was taking care of her seventy-year-old husband, Fred.

Fred had multiple system atrophy, or MSA, which is a rare and devastating disease affecting the nervous system. It is progressive, and over time every system of the body shuts down. He was at the end stages of his disease when we started talking in the summer of 2020, early in the COVID-19 pandemic. He had been bedbound for over a year and a half at that point, his hands so contracted that Lily had to work hard to keep his nails clipped, lest the force of his nails on his palms broke through his skin.

The only help Lily and Fred had was from certified nursing assistants, or CNAs, paid for by Medicare's hospice program. This is one of the types of home healthcare coverage Medicare offers within specific, limited circumstances, but the shifts were short, maybe thirty minutes, three times a week, to take care of specific tasks. When the hospice nurse came by once a week, she took Fred's vitals, performed wound care, and changed his catheter. That nurse also checked his urine and looked for any bedsores.

At the most recent check, he had one. "He's been getting more bedsores now, and now we have to put a big bandage on it," Lily tells me.

The rest of the time, Lily was doing the care, all day and all night. The demands were intense and relentless. She set up a workstation, which was a large folding table piled high with Chux (absorbent pads you put underneath someone in bed), ointments and bandages for bedsores, wipes, antibacterial cleaners, latex gloves, swabs for his mouth, and catheter supplies, among other things.

As part of her routine, she would bathe Fred a couple of days after the nurse visit. As she described her ritual to me, she said, "I get a little tub of water, a basin, I'll bring it back with two washcloths. I'll have the baby wipe things. Then I'll have little square cloths, white—what do you call those? They're very soft. They're an extra little wipe-up tool I have."

She carries the basin to his room, along with the wipes, cloths, and she'll also line up paper towels. "I like to use those too, especially if he has smeared feces inside of his groin, on his testicles." And then she'll lift his legs up. "I'll put his feet up on myself, and his legs are so heavy he can't hold them up. They eventually go down, because he can't control that." Often, she'll get started and have to say to him, "'Fred,' I say, 'I have to cut your hair again on your testicles, because there's a lot of dingleberries down here.'"

As she holds his legs up, she'll go in with the warm water and the wipes to get out whatever feces she can. Then she lays him flat and lifts his right leg over the top of his left ankle. She does this so she can turn him onto his side. "I have a little pillow for him to rest his head on while I turn him to the left. I make sure I have all the materials I need. The cleaning materials are on the bed right smack next to me. . . . Then I wipe him again that way, in that direction. Then while he's lying on that side, I put a Chux down."

She'll slide the Chux up underneath him on one side and use a long bolster pillow to hold him up. "I get busy cleaning or whatever I have to do. If he has any bedsores, I have to clean them really good and use Desitin or a barrier cream." If the sore is really bad, she'll get the bandage supplies. "The nurses conferred with me the other day that he's got a number two or close to a number three wound. You have to keep that dry, not put anything on it and just put the bandage over it."

Sometimes she'll finish the bath and, "I'll have him totally back on his back and he'll poop again, so then you'll have to do it all over again."

This is when she goes outside of herself. "That's when I start singing and making up operas, funny songs, funny things I do." And then she'll do it all again, the wiping, the cream, the Chux, the bolster pillow, lifting the legs. She does as many glove changes as she needs, and when it's all over, she hums as she cleans up the piles of litter that have accumulated on the floor.

———

As I listened to Lily talk, my mind brought up some of the more difficult memories I had caring for J. One morning in 2010, nearly four years after her bone marrow transplant, we were having breakfast together in our apartment. She was trying to drink water out of a cup. She had become increasingly weak from the extreme effects of congestive heart failure and chronic GVHD, a disease sometimes acquired from bone marrow transplants, where the transplanted immune system attacks the host body. She'd made it through multiple major issues over the years, including a colon resection when a tumor was found, ongoing GVHD, cardiac events, and psychotic episodes from the effects of all that prednisone.

J tentatively propped her cup between her rigid fingers and brought it carefully to her mouth. The GVHD had sclerosed her hands so much that her fingers were stuck rigidly straight, her palms permanently collapsed. But she tipped her head just a little too far back. And what is the word? What is the sound of a head flopping back, collapsing at the top of the spine? Her head hung heavy in the wrong direction, her neck splayed back, overstretched, the skin pulling. I jumped up as soon as I saw it. Her gaze was forced to the ceiling, and she emitted a weak, shaking croak.

"Laura, help."

She did not have the strength to lift her head back. I ran to put my hands on the back of her head, gently raising it.

The horror of this couldn't stand on its own, however, because it was just another terrifying moment in a sea of them. It had been more than four years since I first brought her home from her transplant in 2006. Little did I know that things would begin their terrifying turn so early. Because a couple of days after she came home, she developed a stomachache and fever. I helped her from her bed to the bathroom. She was so shockingly thin. After helping her onto the toilet, I went to call the hospital, because a fever meant going to the emergency room. But then she was moaning.

When I peered into the bathroom, I saw her, bald, emaciated, slumped. The port at the top of her skull, used to deliver chemo directly into her central nervous system, protruded under her scalp like a cyclops eye. Her torso leaned slightly to her right, toward the tiled wall; she was unable to hold herself in an upright position. And there was blood everywhere. It had filled the toilet and sprayed onto the floor, the seat, and the wall. It was a jarring visual, blood snaking into the grout of the white tiles. The intense color. The spatter, the smell. Eventually, she was bleeding out and sliding down, slithering onto the bathroom floor as I tried to catch her.

My heart beat furiously, instinctively, and foolishly, thinking it could pump enough blood for the both of us. I tried to conceal my panic. I picked her up and held her as we made our way back to bed. But a minute later, she was back in the bathroom again shitting copious amounts of blood. I wiped it up, put clothes on her. I was panicked but cooed to her that everything would be okay, that I would get her to the hospital.

I got her up and out the door to her car. I used my calming voice, even as I was walking urgently, holding her frail body up to carry as much of her ninetysomething pounds of weight as I could.

I wrangled her into the front seat, and we sped northward toward the Queensboro Bridge, rhythmically clicking ourselves over the grating, hurling ourselves across the East River to the Upper East Side. She was immediately admitted, given two units of blood, and sedated.

———

When I talked to caregivers across the country, I was not surprised that traumatic events were part of their story, just one after another and another. Even if people did not explicitly say they felt traumatized, over and over I noticed things that indicated trauma, such as their flat affect when recounting these events. Many would describe a horrific scene in an eerie—but recognizable to me—monotone; I homed in on their resignation and detachment, seeing myself and others I'd heard talk over the years in them.

Other times the trauma manifested in a rush of feelings. One man I spoke to described how out of control his anger felt at times. "You've got to step back, and if you don't step back enough, you jump off the cliff. It's that simple," he told me. Another yelled at me over the phone during nearly the entire interview. He wasn't yelling at *me* per se but rather yelling about what was happening to him and his wife, who had experienced a devastating stroke. His rage was right there, blanketing every surface.

Other interviews were characterized by profound sadness and easy-to-come tears. While some numbly provided harrowing details and others yelled, there were also those who simply wept. And then there was the disorientation. Some people told their stories in circular and confusing timelines, mixing up years and events. I remember one woman searching for affirmation while talking to me, repeatedly asking if she sounded silly or if she was making sense. *No, you do not sound silly*, I would say softly. *Yes, you are making sense.*

———

From my own experience and the stories of others, it seemed to me that there is specific trauma that arises from caregiving. Of course the consolidation of intensive medical care onto The One begins to fray their mind, pushing them to the edges of their emotional and psychological capacities. Was it any wonder then that people often felt forced to live in "the gray," to make desperate choices like having affairs to preserve their mind, their sense of self?

I once again reached out to Dr. Barry Jacobs, the psychologist. He told me that there is very little research on caregivers and trauma that he knows of, but he believes it is an important topic. One of the few resources I could find was a *New York Times* column he had previously been interviewed for about how he often sees caregivers in his practice who are experiencing flashbacks and other PTSD symptoms. He also wrote an advice column on how caregivers can cope with trauma symptoms. But, he told me, there really wasn't a strong body of research about caregiver trauma for him to draw from.

I went on the hunt and found recent, but still cursory, studies. One literature review on rates of depression, anxiety, and PTSD among family caregivers after a loved one was in the ICU found that the documented prevalence of PTSD ranged from 3 percent to 62 percent. Such a huge range tells us we need to know more. Another review noted that younger caregivers, women, and those with lower incomes were at a heightened risk for PTSD.

I was struck by the absence of studies explicitly considering race in caregiving trauma. As Sami Schalk writes in *Black Disability Politics*, many people of color are disabled by traumatic events, often at the hands of the state, rendering both disability and caregiving even harder to talk about. One heavily cited paper on race and PTSD more broadly (that is, PTSD not necessarily related to caregiving) shows clear disparities along racial lines, with Black people having the highest rates in that study. (It is worth noting that the same study seems to do a poor job accounting for Native Americans, a clear indication of the neglect and violence that these populations have faced and continue to face in the context of health and medicine.) Key here is the enormous gap between who will feel able to safely seek or have access to treatment and who will not. When PTSD affects people of color, it usually goes untreated.

Then I stumbled upon a study of caregivers for patients who had leukemia, which is what J had. The researchers examined symptoms of PTSD in caregiver-patient dyads, which meant the patient was still alive to ask about their experiences, alongside the caregiver. Surprisingly, investigators found that more caregivers than patients met the criteria for PTSD, especially if the caregivers were spouses or parents. In 2025, a new study found that across all the available literature, at least 15 percent of caregivers for someone with cancer had experienced traumatic stress, though it also noted the small sample sizes and lack of diversity in the studies they found.

As I pondered the information from this research and all the stories I was hearing firsthand, I thought about how little we know about the extent to which PTSD affects caregivers. I also thought about the irony of calling a support group for spousal caregivers the Well Spouse Association. Many of us were, in fact, not well at all.

CHAPTER 22

The Split

WHILE WRITING THIS BOOK, I OPENED A BOX THAT HAD been right under my feet for about a decade. For years, I had used it as a footstool under my desk. It was a vintage suitcase made of a very light wood, with a handle, once leather, but which had deteriorated into a soft paper. At some point, I had put all the letters and ephemera from my time with J inside it. I don't remember doing this.

In her 2020 book *Awful Archives*, the scholar Jenny Rice describes different "registers of evidence" that mark and record life. She suggests that some of the evidence of who we are happens at life's very edges. These edges can yield strange, ephemeral, and even weird objects, but the evidence there can nevertheless illuminate our intimate life-worlds. So I began to think of the term *archive* as expansively as possible, as I searched for evidence of myself, my life. I decided to think of what was inside that box under my feet as evidence, as an awful archive that could help me sort out what happened.

I took the crumbling handle and slid the suitcase out from under my desk across the hardwood floor and braced myself. It was stuffed with papers: letters of our heady first days in 2005, dated and still in their envelopes with postal codes stamped on them, and dated notes that span years. I sorted things into two piles: the things I wrote to J, the things she wrote to me.

I inhaled the smell of J's musk that had seeped into everything. I read. It was all gushing; promises of eternity, declarations of need, pleas for understanding. Many were clearly written in the hospital. One scrap of paper with my handwriting said: *I've gone to the family lounge, but I will be right back.* And another in J's shaky handwriting, *They've taken me to X-ray.*

There was a letter I wrote to J in 2010, on the back of a brown paper bag, as if I had been so overcome I had to write it on whatever I could find in an arm's reach. In it, I write that I know she is dying, that I don't know how to say goodbye, but I am trying.

Everything in the box was meticulously dated: a note J left on the kitchen counter in 2007 when we lived that one year on the quiet street in Prospect Heights with the tall trees. *Dinner is in the fridge.* There was a note she had slipped into my lunch bag on my very first day of teaching a college class, a note I wrote to her that I was out walking the dog. So many of our mundane, everyday domestic moments had been mercilessly, relentlessly catalogued and archived.

Lauren Berlant wrote in their book *The Queen of America Goes to Washington City* that what might seem like garbage or "waste materials" in the mundane stuff of everyday life are actually "pivotal documents in the construction, experience, and rhetoric of quotidian citizenship in the United States." So, I used this refuse, these leftovers, these scraps and ephemera to try to locate myself—as best as I could—in those moments, in a system, in a culture, in love.

There were even pictures; a shot taken at a restaurant in Manhattan, another on a trip to Italy. But I cannot remember being in these places; years of my life, I discovered, had been cleanly sliced off from my memory. Occasionally, a gauzy glimpse of something came as I leafed through, but it was fleeting and blurred. Snippets of scenes unfolded outside my body, as though I was watching from afar, choppy and dreamlike. Did J code that night in the emergency department as her body was swallowed up into the murky waters of congestive heart failure, or was I making that up?

To try to get things straight in my mind, to figure out more details of what had happened, I took stock of my very top bookshelf, where the journals I diligently kept all those years collected dust. I dated them and stacked them in chronological order. I began reading at the beginning, 2005. Quickly, I learned that I did not remember writing them or what they contained. And it was not long before the entries began to sound as though they were being written under extreme duress. I triangulated dates of journal entries with outgoing messages in my email. I found elaborate narratives I had written, emails about deeply felt feelings, lots of resolute and very logical-sounding plans for coping. I sounded so strong, so *competent*.

I searched my calendar for the dates in my journals and emails. I thought knowing what things I was doing related to work or school might help me remember. It did not. My curiosity morphed into dread, into a distressing sense that everything would feel foreign forever. These were the archives, the very facts of my life, but I still could not remember.

In the last year of J's life, we had decided to start filming. It was all part of J's penchant for documentation; she wanted to make a video diary, she thought there should be a record of her. But when I watched them now, my stomach pitted in the horror of it all.

There I was, with J, again and again. In one video, I transferred J in a very technical way from lying down to sitting. I counted out pills and monitored her as she swallowed. I did physical therapy exercises with her. I lay in bed with her, cuddling and talking about our feelings about her possible death. In one, we are mourning the sad fact that J will never ride a bicycle over the Manhattan Bridge again.

Saline bags, IV poles, and physical therapy tools littered the frames. There it was—hours upon hours of footage, proof, evidence of us—and all I could do was numbly watch them, only registering the tears on my cheeks when I put my hand up to touch them. Who was that on those videos, in these papers, in those letters? I had no recollection of any of this.

———

PARTITION, *noun*:
1. The action of parting; the state of being parted
2. Something that divides: especially an interior dividing wall
3. One of the parts or sections of a whole

PARTITION, *noun*:
A partition is a section of a storage device, such as a hard disk drive or solid state drive. It is treated by the operating system as a separate logical volume, which makes it function similar to a separate physical device.

———

Being The One split my mind in two. In Judith Herman's classic text, *Trauma and Recovery*, she outlines the key characteristics of trauma and post-traumatic stress disorder. She explains that trauma gives rise to "uncanny alterations of consciousness." Because traumatic events alter the nervous system, memories are "preserved in an abnormal state, set apart from ordinary consciousness." This is why traumatic memories are often lost, warped, fragmented. They get turned into bits and pieces of sensory information—a static image in the mind, a sound, a feeling.

Broadly, these alterations in consciousness are known as dissociation. From a psychological perspective, nothing about my experience is special or unique. My extensive memory loss of these years because of dissociation during them is utterly unremarkable. Memory loss is a common symptom of PTSD.

Though trauma was once thought to be reserved only for understanding experiences outside the ordinary (and what could be more ordinary than the unreliability, the mortality, of our bodies?), we now know this is not true. As Judith Herman makes clear, "Traumatic events are extraordinary, not because they occur rarely, but rather because they overwhelm. . . . Unlike commonplace misfortunes, traumatic events generally involve threats to life or bodily integrity, or a close personal encounter with violence and death. They confront human beings with the extremities of helplessness and terror."

Not everyone who experiences something traumatic develops PTSD, but I did. Having already experienced long-term developmental trauma in childhood prior to knowing J, I was primed for it. I now live with something called complex PTSD or cPTSD. Because there was not just one single event that happened, but rather a prolonged series of events and a years-long state of extreme stress, the effects I live with are more complicated. (That's the "complex" part of it.) One feature of my cPTSD is that my mind erects a permanent wall and pushes many of my memories across it, beyond my reach.

I have spent untold hours out wandering the plains of my memory, patrolling the partition's edges, wondering how to jump the divide. How do I stand at its edge and try to tell the story of what is lost *over there*?

In mid-2010, as more and more terrors unfolded in J's body and mind, I do know that I began to operate on some alternative plane, carving out a secret life, going on internet dates, just to narrate who I was out loud to strangers, never mentioning J to them. I did this over and over again, in some flailing attempt to remind myself of who I was outside of her, outside of what was happening to us, as if I could somehow erase that pain.

Casting shadows of some distant, unrealized version of myself in the light of strangers at a bar from time to time became the only escape I could arrange for. It did and does feel deeply shameful. I slid further and further away from myself, disgusted at my grief and at what I felt I had to do to survive what was happening to J, to me. But these respites also felt like a drug, like the only thing sustaining me so I could keep walking through our apartment door. But there was no escape. I drifted somewhere, increasingly dissociated and absent in my own life. J and I hurt each other more and more, both of us retreating somewhere the other couldn't. And every day, I awoke to her bluish-gray feet sticking out from under the covers at the foot of our bed, her circulation so compromised that they looked like the feet of a corpse. In the mornings, I slowly brought my eyes up from her feet toward her chest, my heart fiercely pumping, wondering if I would know, just from the stillness, that she was dead, hoping I would never have to see her that way.

My experiences with trauma and dissociation and the dynamics of my memory loss influenced how I encountered the people I interviewed for this book. It is what spurred me to find other caregivers and their partners, to craft detailed, systematic questions for them: *What does your typical day look like? What happened and when? Tell me, step-by-step, how do you accomplish care? What do you love about your partner? Tell me, how do you feel about your life, your illness, or your caregiving?* I knew what to ask because of what for me had gone missing. My inquiry became a method of shared experience; mapping the partition required a collective effort.

In these conversations, I met my own past self, over and over again. The more I talked to people, the more memories were triggered. When caregivers I spoke to rattled off medications at lightning speed, I became me again standing at the nurse's station, reciting on command all the meds, dosages, allergies, and a complete medical history along with J's full name and date of birth. I hear myself saying them aloud over the tall counter: *Sirolimus, Vasotec, Edecrin, Plaquenil, Reglan, Remeron* . . .

When I talked to a man in Pennsylvania, he paused abruptly as we were going over the timeline of his wife's illness. She had lupus, rheumatoid arthritis, and several other conditions that caused her chronic pain. It was a years-long trajectory he was trying to lay out for me—but he had left out something, he suddenly told me. It was a crucial detail he had entirely blocked out, but that had come back to him during our conversation.

"She attempted suicide in October of 20— I don't know if it was 2018. I can't remember if it was 2019 now or 2018. I think it was 2019." Disorientation. Time loops. He searched his mind.

"At that time, she was taking an opioid, Oxycontin. I know that the day she attempted suicide I'd just gotten a prescription refilled. She had one hundred and twenty pills and she took all one hundred and twenty Oxycontin."

J had the same impulse, I thought. I had myself forgotten this until that moment, put it away somewhere. Not long after that morning at the breakfast table when her head fell back, J had asked me to kill her. She was propped on the couch, arms rigid and desperately reaching for her pills. She was hysterically ordering me to open the brand-new bottle of Ativan so she could take them all. I tore the bottle from her weak hands and wrapped myself around her flailing sobs, her voice shaking and tears soaking my clothes. I held her as hard as I could, trying to calm this urge in her.

In this man's case, he had gone out to run some errands. His wife was in bed when he got home; this was not unusual. He thought she was resting, so he prepared dinner. As their usual dinnertime approached, he went to wake her up.

"I called to her. She didn't respond. I went in. I shook her and she didn't respond. Then I saw the empty bottle of pills on the tabletop and called 911," he said. And then he numbly changed the subject. I recognized his trauma through remembering my own.

When one woman who cared for her husband told me about being so exhausted in the hospital that she fell asleep standing up in the elevator, I suddenly became me again, curled up in the fetal position on the hard, white linoleum floor of the urgent care department at Memorial Sloan Kettering sometime between the years 2006 and 2010. I registered the feel (rough, starched) and color (white) of a warm blanket from the semisecret blanket warmer the nurses have tucked away in the hallway. I was overcome with the feeling of my dead-tired bones and the dread in my marrow; anytime we ended up here, we were fearing the end.

When I talked to another caregiver who mentioned occasionally using local respite care services, she used the word *reentry* to describe her return home afterward. When her words tumbled out, I was suddenly me again, standing in the stairwell of our apartment building in 2010, avoiding my own reentry. I remembered skipping the elevator to take the stairs whenever I ran a small errand just to extend my time away a few moments longer. I was me again, pausing on the last landing before our door, my body frozen by an overwhelming sense of despair and desperation, of never wanting to walk through that door again, of not wanting to watch her die.

Over and over people shared a cascade of terrors that I felt together with them—a thrashing in the night followed by an airlift; finding your partner on the floor, unconscious; a sudden thud and CPR; a mangled body from a motorcycle accident; the bleeding out of an amputated leg on the floorboard of a car; lingering and ongoing anxiety attacks, panicking on a city bus and having to practically jump out at the next stop, breaking out in a cold sweat at the barbershop for no reason other than the snapping of the cape around the neck somehow taking you back to the moment when you found your wife on that god-awful floor.

———

I think back to Lily bursting into song when it got to be too much for her as she cleaned Fred's body after he had soiled himself again. What songs did she sing? Was she crying while she sang, or had she, like me, ended up somehow so outside of herself that she didn't feel anything anymore?

When Lily let me know that Fred had died and her time caregiving had ended, I wondered if, like me, she had felt disoriented and adrift afterward. Was her mind partitioned too? Would she remember the stories she told me then? Will the other caregivers I spoke to remember the details of theirs? I don't know, but perhaps my conversations with them, and these moments I witnessed and documented in this book, will become awful yet precious records for them—for all of us—too.

Where There Is a History There Is a Future

What we have broken we can mend.
—Octavia Butler, *Parable of the Talents*

I am looking out of the three large windows of my aunt's living room. In the foreground of the view are trees, spindling upward with clumps of three or four leaves left hanging on at the very tip-tops. Behind them rises the Brooklyn Museum. This evening, a fog surrounds it yet again; the hardness and sheer size of the building is masked, barely appearing in the soft gray.

Looking out at it now, I briefly wonder if this is that same patch of fog that J and I had walked into nearly twenty years ago. Maybe all this time. it has been out on its own journey, circling, reconstituting itself again and again. I imagine it making its way along some elaborate route, dragging itself across the hemispheres. And it has, inexplicably, returned now, to sit right in front of me again.

———

I have not told you the story of the end, of how J died. How, after all that J and I endured together, I was not there in the hospital when it finally happened. Instead, I was standing in the hallway of this apartment when I got the call.

I can no longer remember with clarity the details of the time leading up to her death, but my journal entries in those last months repeat the same desperate mantras: *I am miserable. I cannot endure anymore. I cannot watch her die for another minute. I am no longer whole.*

———

Here's what I *can* remember: the beginning of the end. In late 2009, I took a trip, and when my flight landed back at JFK, instead of picking me up in our car, J had somehow managed to drive herself to the ER at Memorial Sloan Kettering while in crisis. She had gone into congestive heart failure and was in mortal danger. I took a taxi, dragging my suitcase with me, straight to the ER.

Everything changed after this. J was hospitalized for weeks, and eventually sent to a cardiac rehab for many more. All of this resulted in a traumatic and rapid deterioration from where she had been prior to her heart failure. Overall, her mobility, strength, and stamina took a nose dive. She could no longer be safely left alone for any period of time.

Meanwhile there was the trouble of my worsening mental health. Her hospitalization and rehab stay lasted about two months, during which I emotionally collapsed. I spiraled into a deep depression, unable to get out of bed or bathe or dress myself. My body and mind seemed to have simply given up, refusing to function. Two friends came over to our apartment, slid clothes on me, and made an emergency appointment with my therapist. I was started on antidepressants and medications for anxiety, and another for sleep.

As J transitioned home after that hospitalization in early 2010, a friend sent emails to our network explaining what was happening to J and encouraging them to sign up to bring meals or walk the dog. I also had to tell J that I needed her to accept the help of home health aides because, quite simply, I was falling apart. At the time, I was still framing the need for paid help as a direct result of my own failures—my inability, in fact, to love her enough to do it all.

She repeatedly set her jaw and said, "I only want you to do it." I will never forget setting her frail body on the toilet, her nuzzling her face against my torso, crying as I stood next to her. She couldn't imagine anyone else doing for her what I was doing, she said. The look on her face ripped me apart.

"I can't. I can't physically or emotionally or logistically do it all. Would you at least try having someone in the house to help?" I asked her.

We applied for home care through Medicaid, but were denied. After nearly six months of appealing, she was finally approved for round-the-clock home care. By that time, in late 2010, the damage to us both had already been done. The number of months it took to get J home care were more than she had left to live. Antidepressants got me out of bed, the sleeping pills got me back in, and in between, a constant flow of anxiety meds made sure the panic attacks weren't incapacitating. It was a blur, a time only of shadows. I begged to talk about end-of-life planning, to face the fact that J was dying, but it seemed to me no one was listening. Or maybe it was that I could no longer perceive their replies.

After years of loving and caring for J, the truth is that I was not there with her when she died. Several weeks before it finally happened, I had moved some of my belongings out of our shared home and into my aunt's apartment on the floor above us—back to where I was living when I first met J. She finally had a home health aide, and others stepped in to share the load. I still wanted to be near her, to help, but I also knew that I could no longer bear to be The One or function mentally or emotionally. By stepping back from being her primary support system, however, I was no longer welcome in J's life in any role. My collapse had hurt her too much. At the time, I understood this rejection to be purely a result of my failures alone. Loving her, it turned out in the end, had not been enough. It broke my heart.

Telling you that I wasn't there when J died is the thing I have been most afraid to tell you. But in truth, I did not endure to the end. I missed the end by several weeks. And twenty years after meeting J, despite all I did and all I sacrificed in the name of love, I still struggle not to feel like I failed. I still predominantly feel shame. If you are a caregiver reading this, I hope you will be kinder to yourself than this.

———

If being The One broke me, then being one of many helped me to heal. As I gathered the stories of other caregivers and disabled people for this book, I came to better understand the impossibility of expecting that one person, however loving, can meet another's every need. I know now that the failure was not all mine, but, at least in part, of a broken, ableist society. In connecting my isolated experience with that of others, I see the possibilities for social repair. I especially learned from queer and disabled people of color who are exploring sustainable ways to meet one another's care needs with skill and imagination.

I spoke with a woman named Nina, whose story, I believe, demonstrates the possibility of securing care in ways that transcend the romantic partnership, that move care work out of the nuclear family and back into the public sphere. When Nina started graduate school in her late twenties, a friend of hers posted a message to an email listserv she was a part of. "I'm thinking of starting a care collective," the friend announced. She was a wheelchair user who needed help with things like showering and transferring to the toilet or bed, and she was searching for people to help meet her day-to-day care needs. Nina, a disabled woman of color, answered her friend's post and suggested they meet to talk about it.

The friend explained what help she needed. Some days she'd need a shower, dinner cooked, and of course help transferring to the toilet when she needed to use the bathroom. Nina, in turn, mostly needed help with her graduate school papers; she could really use someone to copyedit. And this friend could provide that service. So they agreed to keep communication open, to engage in an ongoing negotiation about their respective needs.

"Let's try every Wednesday," Nina suggested as a schedule for her visits. The friend agreed.

Every Wednesday, Nina and her friend texted each other to check in. Every Wednesday evening, Nina went to her apartment.

"It was a bit like hanging out," Nina told me. "I went to my friend's house, and she said, 'Do you want anything to drink?' or 'What do you need today?' Sometimes we'd just chat, other times it was a shower."

And whenever Nina needed copyediting, her friend provided this care in return. It was more like a barter, maybe even "contractual" in a sense, but Nina stresses, "It doesn't mean that I didn't receive anything but copyediting. I certainly received a lot of emotional care from the person. And I had a place to go every week, a place to chill." Over time, Nina says, "I learned, and we grew as it went." Key to this arrangement was that bartering allowed both Nina and her friend to maintain dignity.

There were other people in this care collective as well, each providing care on different days. Nina didn't overlap with the others, but she did get to know them. Her friend would periodically have gatherings so that everyone who was part of the care collective could meet. Each person had a different role, some people were on call, but there was no single person who was The One to do everything; instead, there were many.

I spoke with disability studies scholar Dr. Akemi Nishida, a professor at the University of Illinois Chicago. She is both an expert and a disabled woman of color with her own experiences in care collectives. In her 2022 book *Just Care*, she describes the different ways care collectives and care webs come to be. She spent years on the ground talking with people engaging in collective care, and her book documents these often invisible practices as well as all the possibilities they have. "There are so many different ways people do it, so many different paths," she told me.

Dr. Nishida explained that some people start with a more traditional arrangement, where The One by default is caregiving alone, before the impossibility of these conditions necessitates a slow and intuitive expansion into a more collective model— similar to what had happened with me in the last weeks of J's life. For others, she says, the shared care work is a temporary thing within a particular context, "focused on a moment and space, not long term." Some disabled people she spoke with in her research insist that collective care is everywhere, all the time, because it's just a necessary part of disabled friendship. "Without care we can't hang out together. In that case, it's more informal and organic, it's the only way we can be together, so we take care of each other to do so," she said.

The phenomenon of care collectives was also documented in Leah Lakshmi Piepzna-Samarasinha's 2018 book *Care Work: Dreaming Disability Justice.* The book has become a bible of sorts for those participating in collective care, with history, testimony, and advice—such as not to assume that there's one right way to do it and to know that it doesn't require a huge number of people. It also includes a list of questions to consider for anyone putting together a care web: *What are the best practices that allow the people offering care to offer care well? How will you build in time off and times when people are sick and need a Plan B?*

I also spoke with Dr. Joseph C. Hill, a Black Deaf queer man and cancer survivor, who told me about caring for his elderly parents at times, even while he struggled with his own cancer-related disabilities. "Black people have always been subjected to systemic oppression and trauma. So when disability or illness happens to us, it's different, we just buckle down and carry on. You just have to get through it. It doesn't matter that you're also sick, you still have to care for the others around you who need it. Everyone has something, so you've just got to do it."

Care collectives and webs are part of a more recent movement, led by queer and disabled people of color, called disability justice. It is no accident that the technology of collective care has been developed and mobilized primarily among these communities; these marginalized groups have known all along that the state cannot be trusted to provide care, and thus have organized mutual aid to make up for the lack of care. Indeed, studies consistently show that caregivers of color utilize fewer "formal supports," like programs and supports run by government agencies or caregiving organizations, than white caregivers. Instead, they tend to rely more on what are called "informal supports," like family members and community ties. And for queer people who were once denied access to marriage and the promised security of a traditional nuclear family, the notion that we must find alternative, communal ways to secure love and care, to choose and make our own families with different distributions of care labor, is an intuitive and necessary one.

At the beginning of this book, I described the disability rights movement, which succeeded in moving the United States away from the institutionalization of disabled people and culminated in the legislative win of the Americans with Disabilities Act of 1990, a sweeping civil rights law that prohibits discriminating against disabled people in areas of public life. But as we have seen in the stories in this book, those gains have not adequately addressed the ways in which ableism remains entrenched in ourselves, our culture, and our policies, leaving "'cliff-hangers' that have yet to be resolved" when it comes to ensuring that disabled people get to lead whole lives. This is in part because the disability rights movement typically centered on the experience of white people, the idea being that disability would be more palatable as a social issue if it could be seen as part of white experience. It did not fully acknowledge the ways that ableism is connected to so much more; eugenics and structural racism, alongside the sexism of being entitled to women's emotional and physical labor, have heavily influenced the lack of social safety nets in this country.

Disability history is the history of being denied care, of a world hostile to vulnerability and the very notion of needing care at all. Disability justice, therefore, takes into account the wisdom and survival strategies of people who have endured despite this violent history. And where there is a history, there is a future.

———

As disability justice communities make cultural and practical strides on the ground, others are working within politics to expand the government's response to the care crisis. I spoke to Jason Resendez, president and CEO of the National Alliance for Caregiving, or NAC, who believes people are starting to see that care "shouldn't be a personal struggle; it should be a shared responsibility because we all benefit from care. More and more people are starting to realize this, and a paradigm shift is happening." He described a broad range of advocates across bureaucratic sectors, including those in the childcare, aging, disability, and patient advocacy communities, as part of a political movement: the care movement. It builds upon and is complementary to the work of past and existing disability movements, as well as labor movements advocating for domestic care workers.

Effective public care infrastructure ideas called for by these movements include simple fixes to ease the eligibility burdens of means-tested programs from the Social Security Administration, as well as universal healthcare to help prevent chronic illnesses and disability, universal long-term care to ensure disabled people can live with dignity in their homes, and labor protections that would secure better pay and working conditions for the care workers performing those jobs. Lobbying for increased government funding to pay care workers a living wage is a central concern of the care movement, because it is a key component of the infrastructure disabled people need for their partners and family members to reliably and ethically share the labor of their care. Still, Resendez told me, there's so much more to do in terms of both cultural change and policy change, and that the needed policy changes are enormous. Caregiving "might be an easy issue to connect to, but it's a hard one from a policy standpoint because the investments and programming required are pretty significant," he said.

As I write this, the Trump administration is decimating the federal workforce, dismantling or severely cutting existing programs upon which disabled people and caregivers currently rely. It has already said it is eliminating the Administration for Community Living, an agency that supports disabled and elderly people living in their homes. Now it is threatening drastic cuts to Medicaid, the only federal program that provides long-term home care, and is seeking to weaken the protections against discrimination enshrined in the Americans with Disabilities Act. The Trump administration is justifying the latter as part of its takedown of DEIA programs, referring to diversity, equity, inclusion, and accessibility. This lays bare the reality: Instead of seeing disabled people as valuable and worth integrating into our world, our current political leadership is instead repeating the same old eugenics sins—targeting disabled people and others, like racial minorities, through the denial of care and access to public life.

But like so many others in the disability and care movements, my dream of a better world remains. I firmly believe that to achieve the legislative wins that would change policy and restructure our public systems, we must more closely examine what goes on in our private lives and in our most intimate spaces. Publicly funded infrastructure can be an antidote to ableism, but building it requires that we truly confront it within ourselves and in each other, in order to reimagine a politics of love and relationships that includes mutual interdependence and collective care.

While disability justice communities have been creating their own infrastructures, most disabled people and caregivers I spoke to are not yet aware of these possibilities, nor are many aware that such communities and movements exist. Most have not been taught or told that they are deserving of care and do not have to be ashamed of asking for it, that they deserve relief from trying to do it all on their own, that care is not solely the responsibility of a partner, and that we can lean on people beyond the nuclear family.

As the stories in this book show, internalized ableism siphons off our capacity to sustainably love one another because it makes us feel ashamed of what we need. This may be especially true of romantic relationships, but this sense of shame we carry about dependency damages all kinds of kinships. When we normalize the belief that true love is about finding that one perfect person, we foreclose opportunities for greater connectivity, and therefore, care. Rather than insisting on the primacy of marriage, there is so much more possibility in cultivating *community*: investing in one another would allow us to better give and receive care, whether between romantic partners, family members, friends, or neighbors. Because when we share each other's pain, our burdens get smaller—*that's* real love. And real love needs public support to flourish. In the future, our vows of love do not have to be a promise to be The One to endure it all alone; instead there is strength in numbers, and we can vow to protect one another as a collective, as a community, regardless of our relation to one another, in sickness and in health.

I believe the more we share our private pain and communicate our needs around disability and care with one another, the more practiced we become at seeing our worth. And when this happens, the clearer it will become that what's at stake with the care crisis is not just lost wages and hours of paperwork, but the very sense that we, every one of us, deserves to live. That there is no shame in needing care and asking others for help. The more we tell our stories, the clearer it will also become that our shame isn't the result of not being good enough or strong enough or loving enough, but of the decisions of a government that refuses to invest in our well-being.

If the state has abandoned us, then we must not abandon each other. We must grow our own care collectives in the absence of publicly funded resources. And we must learn to truly love ourselves—and one another—enough to accept our bodies with all their vulnerabilities, using this love to grow ever stronger in our demands for the care infrastructure we deserve.

————

America's care crisis descends from a history of eugenic violence, and that violence is still playing out every day, in private moments behind closed doors. In order to move toward a different, better future, we must bear witness to these intimate stories. So, let this book be a love letter, an archive, a public record of the pain we have endured alone and the care we owe to one another going forward.

Public Display
of Affection

Dear You,

All the advice out there about how to write a love letter says that the writer should be vulnerable, that they should be coming from a place of deep feeling. I have tried to tell you of my own brokenheartedness, failures, and pain, alongside yours. Together, you and I told our stories to make this book. And I am, let's be honest, emotional about you. There, I said it. I'm smitten by you, your own vulnerability, your willingness to be human with me, to talk about all the difficult things we talked about. I know I shouldn't be. I know I'm breaking "research rules," but I can't help it.

In interviews, you shared the history of your relationship, of falling in love. Then we talked about the details of your day-to-day life now, even your most intimate daily routines. I visited some of you. You fed me. You gave me a space to sleep. You wrapped me up in your linens (a quilt passed down through generations of your family), you let me witness you, you offered me dinner, early morning coffee, a snack. You set the table and included a seat for me. You invited me to stay for a game of cards. You told me your secrets. You made me fruit salad. You made me pasta. You sent photos and well-wishes. You emailed me to make sure I got home.

You are each the impetus for this love letter. Whether you are a caregiver or you are the person cared for (and let's face it, we are often both), you moved me. I am emotional about you. This is my public love letter to you. To my most beloved fellow humans with a body: I want the world to see your value. I hope this public display of affection opens the possibility for a shift from "I care" to "we care." Let us, in this public declaration of love, scale up. We can build relationships with one another as we read together, out loud, our love letter.

———

The first time you and I spoke, I saw you onscreen, your camera angled down at you from a high shelf. Like so many other participants, you looped around in your story, time folding in on itself over and over. You held so much information in your head—medications and treatments, hospitalization dates.

You told me about your affair. You told me about the feeling of being held, the feeling of being attended to, just for a short while. You were rejuvenated. You also told me, quickly and profusely, that you love your husband, but that you were dying inside. I heard the distance you held inside you, between what you really wanted—for this not to be happening—and what you must do to survive it. Later, you sent me photos, and I could see how you caressed him. Multiple times a day, you suctioned his mucus. We looked at pictures of the suction machine together and talked about it. You sent me photos of him gaunt, gray. But you also sent photos of the two of you happy, cheeks pressed together and wrinkled, smiling.

What is the shape of love? How expansive can it be? You said you sometimes have to leave his world, but you come back, again and again. You see, you told me, there is nothing wrong with his heart or his lungs, so this could go on for years. But you also told me you know that if anyone knows, you will no longer be worthy of love. You will no longer be worthy of care, despite all the care this world has asked you to give without giving anything back to you. And so you told no one.

I too did things I'm ashamed of to survive. I too sit with the monster that is weaponized regret. I ask again: What is the shape of love? How expansive can it be? To care is complicated. To receive it is too. All I can think now is that there are so many rules and assumptions that it can break us, limit us in what we consider to be the shape of love. I did not say any of this to you on the phone, but I felt a profound sadness and a longing to comfort you. I saw you in all of your cognitive dissonance, in all of the struggle. I held it close and sat with it. At the end of that call, you said, in your confession voice again, that you felt like a bad person. But I did not see a bad person. You were just trying to fill the well, trying to keep it all together. And I want you to know, you were not the only one who made such a confession to me. There were so many more of you than you might imagine.

————

You told me about falling asleep in the elevator. You were on the other side of your own cancer treatment, and trying to keep your husband alive. But you were so tired you couldn't even make it the few floors up to your husband's hospital room before falling asleep standing up, right there in the elevator. And then you took a deep breath and told me harrowing and gruesome details of cleaning your husband's recurring wounds, which are so deep that his tendons are often exposed. You are alone, fighting, slashing, and marching your exhausted body through not just the blood and gore but also the mountains of insurance paperwork. I see you falling apart and yet you cannot because there are no other options. I don't want to let go of your metaphorical hand from a distance. Do you know this? You may not know that I am thinking of you, but I am.

———

When you and I got on the phone to talk about how we were going to be having calls together, the first question you asked me was if you counted. You asked me if you were eligible to tell your story. "Do I do enough?" you wondered out loud to me. You doubted your legitimacy. "Other people have it worse, I'm sure of it," you said.

Almost every single one of you—caregivers and sick or disabled folks alike—said some version of this to me. You gave all kinds of reasons as to why what you do is nothing of import, or is less than what others do, so how could you and your story possibly count or be interesting? This is often an impulse people have, this need to diminish what's happening to them, because it is a way to cope with their trauma. But also these are the stories of our lives, and it is in these stories, in the everyday, that the power of the world to crush us is made clear, as is your power to withstand, to fight back, to thrive. It is in the everyday that I want you to see the glory that is your survival.

So when you say these self-denigrating things to me, I think about what it means to listen to you, to care for you when you tell me things like this. I didn't say it then, but it is my urge now to tell you that you don't need to feel like your experience is any less than anyone else's. I want you to value what you know, what you do, who you are, and appreciate how you are trying to navigate being a human with a body and a mind. We all have our breaking points. You are allowed yours.

You were slow in unfurling your life in front of me, since you weren't sure it counted. You worried that you were complaining too much. But I sat with you quietly. I listened, in the event you wanted to talk, wanted to tell me more. Because you do count. You do matter. Your exhaustion is real, your pain is real, your anger valid. It is oh so tiring to carry what society has abandoned you with. Our bodies, our minds, they sometimes fail us. It is a loss. And in each of you, I saw someone who was simply trying to bring their full self to that reality.

When you and I sat together, things started to come out. I witnessed your bravery, your fierceness as you sat in your own story, as we traveled back to when you met each other, how you fell in love. You wept for an hour, talking quietly through tears, both of us dabbing our eyes. Your pain was close, right there in the front, just waiting for a small crack in the door to seep out. You told me in a text message that after our first conversation you felt so vulnerable. I am writing to you now in awe of your vulnerability.

You asked me if what you were saying was silly or stupid. Then, as you unfolded everything in your life, in your story, you began to give yourself permission to feel the pain of what had happened. I hope you saw then and know now that what you have to say is not silly or stupid. So many of you, as you talked, began to say to me, wow, I didn't realize I did all that. You started to see its worth.

For many of you, you talked simply because I asked. It seemed that no one had asked you questions like this before. You were not practiced at this. You asked me if you were making sense because you jumped around in time so much, your life spiraling in time over and over, warping your sense of when things happened. You tried to get the years right. You worried you sounded nonsensical. You did not. And I told you so.

You asked, "Do I count?" not because you doubted your experience, but because you doubted your legitimacy. "I have a same-sex partner, so maybe it doesn't count," you surmised. You weren't sure I held your relationship in the esteem it deserves. Yes! You count! Your relationship is valid. In fact, I am one of you.

———

I hold close in my memory the pictures you sent me that were so saturated with light, the sun streaming in through the bedroom windows onto your husband's hospital bed bleached out the images. Your pictures were overexposed, as are we, as are you. The harsh colors of the objects, of the medical equipment, faded out in this overexposure and there was a flattening, in that light, of the scene. I heard your flat affect, how your voice was pummeled into a soft squeak. I saw myself and my story in yours; I recognized your confusion. I remembered the times I was so out of my mind with grief that I got lost in my own neighborhood. I felt your lostness too. You are not alone. I know you feel you are falling apart and yet you cannot because there are no other options. This is my love letter to you, to try and be one small thing to hold you up.

———

You were convinced you were a waste. You told me about how badly you did not want to be "one of them." You did not want to be friends with the other kids with a disability like yours. You told me about practically being knocked down in the grocery store while you held your cane, people brushing past you, unthinkingly, too close. Any kind of tipping could throw you off balance. You said people just didn't care. That they stared. You thought you might be pathetic, not worth taking up space in a store, much less being worthy of staying married to. Now that you are no longer earning a paycheck, you thought you were just a drain. When you used your disability parking placard, people stared, evaluating you as if they were in a position of authority over you. You wanted them to mind their business, but still, you absorbed their disdain. It stung.

You were seduced by the hatred that seethes all around us, the hatred of precarious, unreliable bodies. It was just too easy for you to believe you were worthless now. And my heart broke. You are not worthless. You are not the burden. You can be disabled, you can be "one of those people" and still be worth something. Has anyone ever told you this? Because you sat there with me in your living room berating yourself. Hours later, we tinkered around in your garage and you showed me how you were finding ways to do things at home, things that I immediately thought other people might want to know. I looked at you and saw brilliance and creativity.

You did not want to become one of them, but you found yourself face-to-face with it. When you talked to me about how it felt, I nodded and listened. But what I really wanted to do was reach across the room and hold you and tell you not to be ashamed. You are not a failure. You're just being asked to make sense of an experience that we don't give people a way to make sense of. The tears fell off your cheeks and onto your shirt. You wiped them with the back of what you called your "good" hand, and I wanted to tell the "bad" side of your body that it was still good too. It is yours, still here, it is you. And you have a unique and valuable way of being in the world that is specific to who you are and the things you love. You love your cats. You love your tools. You love cooking and you love building things. You like to play the slots. You are funny and love to crack jokes. You survived another day in a world that does not make it easy. You are not the worthless person you think you are.

———

You called me from the rehab facility and told me you had gone into heart failure. "Caregiving on my own is killing me. I can't do it all anymore," you said. Your rehab days were spent trying desperately to make sure someone is bringing your husband food. Between the sobbing, you still managed to crack a joke about how maybe your husband can put his laundry in the dishwasher. "That," you said laughing, "he might be able to do."

And you? You raged. You did not rage at me, no, it wasn't directed at me, but you raged. You let it rip, curse words spewing out of your mouth, the spit I could practically hear flying in the air on the other side of the phone. You raged at her illness, at a system that, in your words, is "just so fucked up!" Indeed it is. Your anger exploding let me know that you are still a whole person and that we each carry our sadness in different ways. Yours was rage.

———

Of course, there is still so much I don't know about you. I don't know who you were before it all happened. I don't know the other parts of your lives. And of course, there's so much we don't share: age, location, even political beliefs. But I still feel for you. I still want to care for you. So yes, I am aware of the limits around how we know each other, but I still find myself wanting to reach for you.

At the end of our calls together, you and I acknowledged how hard it all was. You cried tears of relief. I reached across to my own box of tissues next to me. "See?" I said, in solidarity with you. Just before hanging up, you said, "It's hard to say goodbye. We are so intimate now." Yes.

When I left your home, when you hugged me goodbye in the driveway, I relished your body, this body that cares. And when I left your home, you hugged me from your wheelchair in the living room, the morning sun streaming in through the open front door. Your body has magic, even though some people might think it doesn't "work."

Each of you showed me—and can show each other, all of us—so much that I long to give you something in return. So I offer up my love and care for you here, on this page. You may be still so deep in the middle of it all, full of urgent caregiving information, full of your body's sensations and seeming failures. Maybe all of this has taken over the forefront of your mind. Trust me when I tell you that later, you may not remember it all. You may no longer recall the day-to-day, the medication dosages, the treatment plans, the trajectories, what hurt in your body, where the tubes were, where exactly the slice of the nerve happened, or when exactly you started to feel worthless. Pieces of your story may disappear, slip away. But I hope you know that there is so much more to you, so much value in who you are, just being here, in your body, no matter what the rest of the world tells you. I hope this letter helps to hold your story, your record, the magnificent and complicated traces of you.

Love,
Laura

Acknowledgments

I am forever grateful and forever changed by each of you who let me into your lives, answered my questions, and were brave enough to share your stories in this book. I know readers will be too. Thank you.

I could never have made this work without the vision, support, and cheerleading so powerfully and generously given from my incredible agent, Tanya McKinnon. It feels silly, from one writer to another, to say that words can't capture my gratitude for you and my awe of you. But it's true. Thank you for seeing me at my most undeveloped and still thinking that I had potential. Having you in my life has changed me.

This book would not exist without my acquiring editor, Sara Birmingham, and the Ecco team, who believed in it from the very start. A special thanks to my editor, Deborah Ghim—the visionary behind what this book ultimately became. Thank you for caring enough about my work to make it the best version it could be, for guiding me through its metamorphosis, and for your incisive, detailed, and meaningful insights and critiques. You didn't have to do it all as well and as thoroughly as you did, but you did. Thank you for making me into the writer I am today.

This book was generously supported through a New America Fellowship, a grant from the Social Science Research Council, a University of Connecticut Humanities Institute Fellowship, and the University of Connecticut Women's Gender and Sexuality Studies Program. The work also benefited from feedback and friendships I made during workshops at Aspen Autumn Words and the Bread Loaf Writers' Conference. And I am lucky to have worked with Kati Standefer, who shared her knowledge and skills on how to write trauma as safely as possible, despite its harrowing nature and unavoidable peril.

So many people have helped me along the way in ways big and small; it feels impossible to name you all, what an embarrassment of riches to be so blessed with this many friends, supporters, and mentors. Here are some standouts: Simi Linton met with me nearly weekly for years to talk about my vision for the book, my creative process, and the seemingly endless writing and rewriting. My colleagues at UConn supported my work and let me be off in my own little world as much as possible to make this book come to fruition—and speaking of colleagues, Alex Friedus, what a writing buddy you are! Early on, Rachel Adams and Michael Rembis wrote *many* fellowship letters. Emily Rapp Black was an early cheerleader who made me think I might actually be a writer and is the reason I wrote and published my very first personal essay. Steven Thrasher, thank you for taking a look at my query letter and opening doors for me. My dear writing group—Katie Gindlesparger and Clare Mullaney—witnessed this work each week for nearly five years and never missed a chance to tell me to keep going. The Center for Disability Studies at New York University, namely Faye Ginsburg, Mara Mills, and Rayna Rapp, gave me a home to think and write during sabbatical. My fellow New America fellows: I didn't just learn about journalistic reporting and moving ethically through the world from you, I made friends with a group of people who taught me the thrill of being hell-bent on changing this world. To those who work for or volunteer with the Well Spouse Association, especially Laurel Wittman, thank you for your support and for facilitating the contacts that would become many of the stories in this book. My thinking was also greatly enriched from the graduate students who took my seminar on care and disability. And of course, Jennie Goldstein and Valerie Lapinski, I love our friendships, thank you for sustaining me.

I would be remiss not to acknowledge my comrades across the many disability and deaf communities I have had the honor of being a part of, as well as my fellow academics studying disability. You are all most responsible for my thinking about disability and care. It is disabled and deaf folks that have led the way for me, always, and have taught me everything I know. I am humbled by you and hope that I have done our communities justice. Some, but certainly not all, of those interlocutors are: Brenda Brueggemann, Diana Cejas, Doron Dorfman, Rachel Fish, Angela Frederick, Michele Friedner, Shira Grabelsky, Martine Granby, Aimi Hamraie, Sara Hendren, Christine Kelly, Christine Sun Kim, Jina B. Kim, Joseph Hill, Joyce Hom, Lawrence Carter-Long, Angel Miles, Jamelia Morgan, Akemi Nishida, Patricia Ordonez, David Roche, Annie Tan, Bess Williamson, and, most especially, Alice Wong.

Thank you to the childcare providers at Brooklyn's Little Cool School and the New York City Department of Education. Your undervalued and underpaid work of caring for my child day in and day out over these years has made this book possible; you all should be given the world.

Finally, I could not have written this book without the care and support of my partner, Lawrence. This book is as much a labor of your love as it is mine. To you and our beloved Agnes Helen: I love you every day.

NOTES

INTRODUCTION: THE ONE

16 The One is usually, but not always, a woman: AARP and National Alliance for Caregiving, *Caregiving in the United States 2020* (AARP, 2020).

16 Six in ten U.S. adults: "About Chronic Diseases," Centers for Disease Control, October 4, 2024, https://www.cdc.gov/chronic-disease/about/index.html.

16 nearly 29 percent: "Disability Impacts All of Us Infographic," Centers for Disease Control, April 14, 202, https://www.cdc.gov/disability-and-health/articles-documents/disability-impacts-all-of-us-infographic.html.

17 to shift the site of care: K. E. Nielsen, *A Disability History of the United States* (Beacon Press, 2013).

17 sheer magnitude of the caregiving crisis stuns: AARP and National Alliance for Caregiving, *Caregiving in the United States 2020*.

17 Few families can afford: AARP and National Alliance for Caregiving, *Caregiving in the United States 2020*.

17 Family caregivers end up providing roughly 80 percent: "Who Will Provide Your Care?," Administration for Community Living, Department of Health and Human Services, last modified February 18, 2020, https://acl.gov/ltc/basic-needs/who-will-provide-your-care.

17 even while a majority are employed: AARP and National Alliance for Caregiving, *Caregiving in the United States 2020*.

17 This includes nursing homes: "The State of Long-Term Care Financing," Scan Foundation, 2014, https://www.thescanfoundation.org/resources-tools/infographic-the-state-of-long-term-care-financing-long-term-care-spending-in-the-united-states/.

CHAPTER 1: THE CHOICE

29 millions of women in the United States: Jessica Calarco, *Holding It Together: How Women Became America's Safety Net* (Portfolio, 2024).

29 "Other countries have social safety nets": A. H. Petersen, "Other Countries Have Social Safety Nets. The U.S. Has Women," Culture Study, annehelen.substack.com, November 11, 2020, https://annehelen.substack.com/p/other-countries-have-social-safety.

29 whatever insurance existed was privately bought: G. B. Moseley III, "The U.S. Health Care Non-System, 1908–2008," *AMA Journal of Ethics* 10, no. 5 (2008): 324–31, https://doi.org/10.1001/virtualmentor.2008.10.5.mhst1–0805.

29 benefits arms race: Jill Quadagno, *One Nation, Uninsured: Why the U.S. Has No National Health Insurance* (Oxford University Press, 2006).

30 employers can take advantage of various statuses: Quadagno, *One Nation, Uninsured.*

30 responsible for their own healthcare: Colin Crouch, *Will the Gig Economy Prevail?* (Polity, 2019).

30 the average cost of a physical exam: "Doctor Visit Costs," Debt.Org, December 11, 2024, https://www.debt.org/medical/doctor-visit-costs/.

30 37 percent of Americans don't have enough money: *Report on the Economic Well-Being of U.S. Households in 2022–May 2023*, Federal Reserve Board, https://www.federalreserve.gov/publications/2023-economic-well-being-of -us-households-in-2022-expenses.htm last updated June 2, 2023.

CHAPTER 2: FADE TO BLACK

39 emergent ideology of eugenics: Wendy Kline, *Building a Better Race: Gender, Sexuality, and Eugenics from the Turn of the Century to the Baby Boom* (University of California Press, 2005).

39 institutionalized and even sterilized: Rich Remsberg, "Found in the Archives: America's Unsettling Early Eugenics Movement," NPR, June 1, 2011, https:// www.npr.org/sections/pictureshow/2011/06/01/136849387/found-in-the -archives-americas-unsettling-early-eugenics-movement.

40 claims about immigrants and their "bad genes": Gram Slattery and Kristina Cooke, "Donald Trump Says There Are 'a Lot of Bad Genes' Among Migrants in the US," Reuters, October 7, 2024, https://www.reuters.com/world/us/donald -trump-says-there-are-a-lot-bad-genes-among-migrants-us-2024-10-07/.

40 the number of Black people who benefit from federal programs: Arthur Delaney and Ariel Edwards-Levy, "Americans Are Mistaken About Who Gets Welfare," *HuffPost*, February 5, 2018, https://www.huffpost.com/entry /americans-welfare-perceptions-survey_n_5a7880cde4b0d3df1d13f60b.

40 humans with bodies that need care: Jina B. Kim, "Cripping the Welfare Queen: The Radical Potential of Disability Politics," *Social Text* 39, no. 3 (2021): 79–101, https://doi.org/10.1215/01642472-9034390.

40 signed Medicare and Medicaid into law in 1965: Jill Quadagno, *One Nation, Uninsured: Why the U.S. Has No National Health Insurance* (Oxford University Press, 2006).

40 white people are the majority of Medicaid beneficiaries: "Distribution of People Ages 0–64 with Medicaid by Race/Ethnicity, Timeframe: 2023," Kaiser Family Foundation, https://www.kff.org/medicaid/state-indicator/medicaid -distribution-people-0-64-by-raceethnicity/?currentTimeframe=0&sortModel =%7B%22colId%22:%22Location%22,%22sort%22:%22asc%22%7D.

40 extending access to care to those they deemed undeserving: Jonathan M. Metzl, *Dying of Whiteness: How the Politics of Racial Resentment Is Killing America's Heartland* (Basic Books, 2019).

41 it was disability activists who protested: John Nichols, "Disability-Rights Activists Are the Real Heroes of the Health-Care Fight," *The Nation*, July 28, 2017.

41 more likely to be working in the gig economy: Risa Gelles-Watnick and Monica Anderson, "Racial and Ethnic Differences Stand Out in the U.S. Gig Workforce," Pew Research Center, December 15, 2021, https://www.pewresearch.org/short-reads/2021/12/15/racial-and-ethnic-differences-stand-out-in-the-u-s-gig-workforce/.

CHAPTER 3: DISCHARGED

45 "the expense of human dignity": Sara Luterman, "It's Time to Abolish Nursing Homes," *The Nation*, August 11, 2020.

45 the quality of care that people may receive in facilities: Joe Eaton, "Who's to Blame for the 100,000 COVID Dead in Long-Term Care?," AARP, December 3, 2020, http://www.aarp.org/caregiving/health/info-2020/covid-19-nursing-homes-who-is-to-blame.html.

45 lower staff-to-patient ratios result in better care and outcomes: Eric Jutkowitz et al., "Effects of Nurse Staffing on Resident Outcomes in Nursing Homes: A Systematic Review," *Journal of the American Medical Directors Association* 24, no. 1 (2023): 75–81, https://dci.org/10.1016/j.jamda.2022.11.002.

45 most Americans don't want to be in a facility: Dennis Thompson, "Americans Over 50 Want to 'Age in Place' at Home, but Many Aren't Prepared: Poll," HealthDay.com, April 13, 2022, https://www.healthday.com/health-news/caregiving/4-13-americans-over-50-want-to-age-in-place-at-home-but-most-aren-t-prepared-poll-2657123727.html.

47 isn't understood as a social experience or political issue: Michael Oliver, "Theories of Disability in Health Practice and Research," *British Medical Journal* 317, no. 7170 (1998): 1446–49.

CHAPTER 4: DECERTIFIED

54 largest safety-net program: *Annual Statistical Report on the Social Security Disability Insurance Program, 2023*, Social Security Administration, October 2024, https://www.ssa.gov/policy/docs/statcomps/di_asr/index.html.

54 nearly a third (29 percent) were receiving less than $1,000: Justin Schweitzer, Emily DiMatteo, and Nick Buffie, *How Dehumanizing Administrative Burdens Harm Disabled People*, Center for American Progress, December 5, 2022, https://www.americanprogress.org/article/how-dehumanizing-administrative-burdens-harm-disabled-people/.

54 By 2025, the average monthly SSDI benefit: "Selected Data from Social Security's Disability Program," Disabled Worker Average Benefits, 1996–2025, Social Security Administration, https://www.ssa.gov/oact/STATS/dib-g3.html.

55 "the benefit applicant is truly biologically incapable": Beatrice Adler-Bolton and Artie Vierkant, *Health Communism: A Surplus Manifesto* (Verso, 2022).

56 The SSA denies about 66 percent: "SSI Annual Statistical Report, 2020: Outcomes of Applications for Disability Benefits," Social Security Administration, https://www.ssa.gov/policy/docs/statcomps/ssi_asr/2020/sect10.html.

56 people who hired lawyers: "Social Security Disability: Additional Measures and Evaluation Needed to Enhance Accuracy and Consistency of Hearings Decisions," U.S. Government Accountability Office, December 7, 2017.

56 processed applications within 110 to 120 days: Sharon Jayson, "Why Social Security Disability Claims Are Taking So Long," AARP, January 17, 2024, updated June 12, 2024, https://www.aarp.org/retirement/social-security /info-2024/disability-claim-wait-times.html.

56 "customer service crisis": Natalie Alms, "30,000 Died in Fiscal 2023 Waiting for Disability Decisions from Social Security," Nextgov.com, April 17, 2024, https://www.nextgov.com/digital-government/2024/04/30000-died-fiscal -2023-waiting-disability-decisions-social-security/395796/.

56 "takes a serious toll" on disabled people: Elizabeth F. Emens, "Disability Admin: The Invisible Costs of Being Disabled," *Minnesota Law Review* 105 (2021): 2329–77.

58 the rates of long COVID: Laura Mauldin, "Long COVID Leaves Newly Disabled People Facing Old Barriers—A Sociologist Explains," *The Conversation*, March 10, 2022, http://theconversation.com/long-covid-leaves -newly-disabled-people-facing-old-barriers-a-sociologist-explains-175424.

59 the "disability con": Ellen Samuels, *Fantasies of Identification: Disability, Gender, Race* (New York University Press, 2014).

59 popular meme of a woman in a wheelchair: Doron Dorfman, "Fear of the Disability Con: Perceptions of Fraud and Special Rights Discourse," *Law & Society Review* 53, no. 4 (2019): 1051–91.

59 we often require disability to be visible: Rachel Carrington, "Stop Assuming I'm Not Disabled Just Because I Don't 'Look Disabled,'" Rooted in Rights, January 8, 2020, https://rootedinrights.org/stop-assuming-im-not-disabled -just-because-i-dont-look-disabled/.

CHAPTER 5: BETTER FRIENDS THAN PEOPLE

64 ingenious methods for getting things done: Arseli Dokumaci, *Activist Affordances: How Disabled People Improvise More Habitable Worlds* (Duke University Press, 2023).

65 watching Ángel show me his hacks: Liz Jackson, "We Are the Original Lifehackers," Opinion, *New York Times*, May 30, 2018, https://www.nytimes .com/2018/05/30/opinion/disability-design-lifehacks.html.

65 different, more expansive ways of being and doing: Aimi Hamraie and Kelly Fritsch, "Crip Technoscience Manifesto," *Catalyst* 5, no. 1 (2019): 1–33, doi: 10.28968/cftt.v5i1.29607.

65 an object might be completely, and ingeniously, reinvented: Laura Mauldin, "Care Tactics: Hacking an Ableist World," TheBaffler.com, no. 64, July 2022, https://thebaffler.com/salvos/care-tactics-mauldin.

65 Disabled people are: "Episode 5: Contra* Straw Ban with Alice Wong,"
    *Contra** (podcast), Critical Design Lab, October 30, 2024, https://www
    .criticaldesignlab.com/podcast/episode-5.

CHAPTER 7: ON HIGH ALERT

83 patients of color routinely receive poorer medical care: A. Gangopadhyaya,
    "Black Patients Are More Likely Than White Patients to Be in Hospitals
    with Worse Patient Safety Conditions," Robert Wood Johnson Founda-
    tion, March 1, 2021, https://www.rwjf.org/en/insights/our-research/2021/03
    /black-patients-are-more-likely-than-white-patients-to-be-in-hospitals
    -with-worse-patient-safety-conditions.html.

83 not listened to about their care needs: Tressie McMillan Cottom, "Why
    Are Pregnant Black Women Viewed as Incompetent?," *Time*, January 8,
    2019, https://time.com/5494404/tressie-mcmillan-cottom-thick-pregnancy
    -competent/.

83 Black people having higher pain tolerances: Deirdre Cooper Owens, *Medical
    Bondage: Race, Gender, and the Origins of American Gynecology* (University of
    Georgia Press, 2017).

83 similar myths about Indigenous and other people of color: Joanna Bourke, "Pain
    Sensitivity: An Unnatural History from 1800 to 1965," *Journal of Medical
    Humanities* 35, no. 3 (2014): 301–19, https://doi.org/10.1007/s10912-014-9283-7.

86 "the concept of for-profit health-care corporations": "Medicaid Managed
    Care for People with Disabilities: Policy and Implementation Considerations
    for State and Federal Policymakers," National Council on Disability, March
    13, 2013, https://www.ncd.gov/report/medicaid-managed-care-for-people
    -with-disabilities/.

87 "Managed care is not about managing care": Teresa L. Scheid, "Managed Care,
    Managed Dollars, Managed Providers: Ethical Dilemmas in Mental Health
    Care," *HEC Forum* 14, no. 2 (2022): 99–118, doi: 10.1023/A:1020951513871.

87 complicating and fracturing the care we receive: Lauren Coleman-Lochner,
    "Private Equity Owns 30% of For-Profit Hospitals, Tracker Says," Bloomberg
    .com, April 19, 2023, https://www.bloomberg.com/news/articles/2023-04-19/
    private-equity-is-buying-struggling-hospitals-is-that-part-of-the-problem.

CHAPTER 8: THE BLUE GLOVES

93 including dissatisfaction with care: Steven Epstein, *Impure Science: AIDS,
    Activism, and the Politics of Knowledge* (University of California Press, 1996).

PART III: NO GOOD MOVES

113 Park McArthur and Constantina Zavitsanos, "Other Forms of Convivial-
    ity," *Women & Performance: A Journal of Feminist Theory*, October 20, 2013,
    https://www.womenandperformance.org/ampersand/ampersand-articles
    /other-forms-of-conviviality.html.

CHAPTER 12: THE TUTOR

122 internalized ableism: Arielle Silverman, "Contending with Ableism from Internalized Ableism to Collective Action," *Ableism* (John Wiley & Sons, 2019), 220–65, https://doi.org/10.1002/9781119142140.ch6.

123 feelings of worthlessness: Kathleen R. Bogart et al., "Disability Pride Protects Self-Esteem Through the Rejection-Identification Model," *Rehabilitation Psychology* 63, no. 1 (2018) 155–59, https://doi.org/10.1037/rep0000166.

123 intersects with other aspects of their lives: Sami Schalk, *Black Disability Politics* (Duke University Press, 2022).

123 avoided as potential romantic partners: Mirabelle Miron et al., "Online Dating for People with Disabilities: A Scoping Review," *Sexuality and Disability* 41, no. 1 (2023): 31–61.

CHAPTER 14: AROUND THE CLOCK

131 "more than half (56%) of boomers": "Bankers Life Study: Boomers Are More Prepared for Death Than Life—and It's Not Getting Better," BankersLife .com, March 12, 2019.

131 While home health services from Medicare: "7 Things to Know About Medicare and Home Health," National Council on Aging, August 16, 2024, https://www.ncoa.org/article/seven-things-you-should-know-about -medicares-home-health-care-benefit/.

134 $3 trillion in lost wages: Rani Snyder, "Unpaid Family Caregivers Lose $522B in Wages Every Year," Route Fifty, December 21, 2021, https://www.route -fifty.com/health-human-services/2021/12/unpaid-family-caregivers-need -support/360022/.

CHAPTER 15: COUCH LIFE

138 the disability tax: Jasmine E. Harris, "Taking Disability Public," *University of Pennsylvania Law Review* 169, no. 6 (2021): 1681–1749.

138 only about 5 percent: "Accessibility in Housing: Findings from the 2019 American Housing Survey," Office of Policy Development and Research, U.S. Department of Housing and Urban Development, March 17, 2022, https://www.huduser.gov/portal/publications/Accessibility-in-Housing -Report.html.

138 those living in mobile homes: "Accessibility in Housing: Findings from the 2019 American Housing Survey."

139 fewer than one in thirty Americans: Alexander Sammon, "The Collapse of Long-Term Care Insurance," *American Prospect*, October 20, 2020, https:// prospect.org/familycare/the-collapse-of-long-term-care-insurance/.

139 Under the ACA, many states raised their limits: "HHS Poverty Guidelines for 2025," Office of the Assistant Secretary for Planning and Evaluation, Department of Health and Human Services, 2025, http://aspe.hhs.gov/topics /poverty-economic-mobility/poverty-guidelines.

140 National Strategy to Support Family Caregivers: "2022 National Strategy to Support Family Caregivers," Administration for Community Living, http://acl.gov/CaregiverStrategy.

140 the Trump administration announced: Julia Métraux, "RFK Jr. Moves to Close Administration for Community Living," *Mother Jones*, March 28, 2025, https://www.motherjones.com/politics/2025/03/rfk-hhs-acl-community-living-shutdown/.

142 known as the "marriage penalty": Sara Luterman, "Marriage Could Mean Losing Life-Saving Benefits for People with Disabilities. So They're Protesting," The 19th, September 13, 2023, https://19thnews.org/2023/09/disability-advocates-marriage-equality-commitment-ceremony/.

143 known as a Medicaid divorce: "Should You Consider a Medicaid Divorce When One Spouse Requires Care and One Does Not?," American Council on Aging, last updated June 4, 2025, https://www.medicaidplanningassistance.org/medicaid-divorce/.

143 About 90 percent of adults over fifty want to age in place: Dennis Thompson, "Americans over 50 Want to 'Age in Place' at Home, but Many Aren't Prepared: Poll," HealthDay.com, April 13, 2022, https://www.healthday.com/health-news/caregiving/4-13-americans-over-50-want-to-age-in-place-at-home-but-most-aren-t-prepared-poll-2657123727.html.

144 In 2022, the turnover rate: Andrew Donlan, "After 3-Year Dip, Home Care Turnover Soars To 77%," Home Health Care News, May 24, 2023, https://homehealthcarenews.com/2023/05/after-dipping-for-three-years-home-care-turnover-rate-soared-to-77-in-2022/.

144 predicts the demand for home health aides: Occupational Outlook Handbook: Fastest Growing Occupations, U.S. Bureau of Labor Statistics, last updated April 18, 2025, https://www.bls.gov/ooh/fastest-growing.htm.

144 This workforce is primarily made up of women of color: E. Haines, "The New Deal Devalued Home Care Workers. Advocates Hope New Legislation Can Undo That," The 19th, October 6, 2021, https://19thnews.org/2021/10/home-care-workers-new-deal-reconciliation/.

145 we have opted to create markets out of caregiving: Beatrice Adler-Bolton and Artie Vierkant, *Health Communism: A Surplus Manifesto* (Verso, 2022).

CHAPTER 16: TO MOVE IS TO HOLD A WE

152 "Access intimacy is that elusive": Mia Mingus, "Access Intimacy, Interdependence and Disability Justice," Leaving Evidence, April 12, 2017, https://leavingevidence.wordpress.com/2017/04/12/access-intimacy-interdependence-and-disability-justice/.

157 The Hoyer lift was invented: David Lykins, "The Man Behind the Hoyer Lift," Med Mart, March 30, 2021, https://medmartonline.com/blog/the-man-behind-the-hoyer-lift/.

159 dealing with another person's urine or feces: Julia Kristeva, *Powers of Horror: An Essay on Abjection* (Columbia University Press, 1982).

159 the "patient lifting equipment" market: *Patient Lifting Equipment Market*, Markets and Markets, 2019, https://www.marketsandmarkets.com/Market -Reports/patient-lifting-equipment-market-178316146.html.

160 When we frame people's needs: Martha C. Nussbaum, *Hiding from Humanity: Disgust, Shame, and the Law* (Princeton University Press, 2004).

CHAPTER 17: FIX IT

165 California, where more than 20 percent of nurses are Filipina: Joanne Spetz, Lela Chu, and Lisel Blash, "Diversity of California's Nursing Workforce Chartbook," University of California San Francisco, January 1, 2018, https://healthforce.ucsf.edu/publications/diversity-california%E2%80%99s -nursing-workforce-chartbook-2018.

165 global care chain phenomenon: Rhacel Salazar Parreñas, *Servants of Globalization: Women, Migration, and Domestic Work* (Stanford University Press, 2001).

167 overwhelming impulses to gamble or shop: Gabriella Santangelo, Paolo Barone, Luigi Trojano, and Carmine Vitale, "Pathological Gambling in Parkinson's Disease. A Comprehensive Review," *Parkinsonism & Related Disorders* 19, no. 7 (2013): 645–53, https://doi.org/10.1016/j.parkreldis.2013.02.007.

CHAPTER 18: A GOOD WIFE

173 there is no other choice: AARP and National Alliance for Caregiving. "Caregiving in the United States 2020," May 14, 2020, https://www.aarp.org/pri /topics/ltss/family-caregiving/caregiving-in-the-united-states/.

174 women and femmes in families as "the Wife": Jina B. Kim, "Against the Wife: Abolishing Romance and Family, Practicing Disability Love-Politics," Dilettante Army, Spring 2023, https://dilettantearmy.com/articles/against-the -wife-abolishing-romance-and-family-practicing-disability-love-politics.

175 men leave their sick wives: Michael J. Glantz et al., "Gender Disparity in the Rate of Partner Abandonment in Patients with Serious Medical Illness," *Cancer* 115, no. 22 (2009): 5237–42, https://doi.org/10.1002/cncr.24577.

175 more socialized to and expected to carry it all: P. H. Collins, *Black Feminist Thought: Knowledge, Consciousness, and the Politics of Empowerment* (Routledge, 2000).

175 a wife, mother, and also breadwinner: Valerie Francisco-Menchavez, *The Labor of Care: Filipina Migrants and Transnational Families in the Digital Age* (University of Illinois Press, 2018).

176 how important family commitment and caregiving is: Julian Chun-Chung Chow et al., "Types and Sources of Support Received by Family Caregivers of Older Adults from Diverse Racial and Ethnic Groups," *Journal of Ethnic and Cultural Diversity in Social Work* 19, no. 3 (2010): 175–94, https://doi.org /10.1080/15313204.2010.499318.

176 the majority report depression: "Caregiver Health," Family Caregiver Alliance, 2006, https://www.caregiver.org/resource/caregiver-health/.

CHAPTER 19: NO SAINT

180 the caregiver's perception of the relationship shifts: Doris Svetlik et al., "Declines in Satisfaction with Physical Intimacy Predict Caregiver Perceptions of Overall Relationship Loss: A Study of Elderly Caregiving Spousal Dyads," *Sexuality and Disability* 23, no. 2 (2005): 65–79, http://doi.org/10.1007/s11195–005–4670–7.

180 taking on a parent-like role: Meredith Jackson, "Attitudes Towards Infidelity in Spousal Caregivers" (Ph.D. diss., University of Minnesota, Minneapolis, 2015).

182 "Chronic grief can feel scary": Marion Cohen, *Dirty Details: The Days and Nights of a Well Spouse* (Temple University Press, 1996).

182 the declining mental health of the caregiver: Jackson, "Attitudes Towards Infidelity in Spousal Caregivers."

183 younger caregiving spouses experience these changes: Jeremy B. Yorgason, Alan Booth, and David Johnson, "Health, Disability, and Marital Quality: Is the Association Different for Younger Versus Older Cohorts?," *Research on Aging* 30, no. 6 (2008): 623–4, https://www.researchgate.net/publication/249630762 _Health_Disability_and_Marital_Quality_Is_the_Association_Different _for_Younger_Versus_Older_Cohorts.

183 they feel they must either change: Marie Y. Savundranayagam and Rhonda J. V. Montgomery, "Impact of Role Discrepancies on Caregiver Burden Among Spouses," *Research on Aging* 32, no. 2 (2010): 175–99, doi: 10.1177/0164027509351473.

183 a taboo topic: B. R. Keene, "A Study of Extramarital-Intimate Relationships of Older Adult Caregivers of Chronically Ill Spouses" (Ph.D. diss., Mississippi State University, Starkville, 1995).

184 "unacknowledged assumptions about the ability to have sex": Tobin Siebers, *Disability Theory* (University of Michigan Press, 2008).

185 everything can be negotiated: Leah Lakshmi Piepzna-Samarasinha, *Care Work: Dreaming Disability Justice* (Arsenal Pulp Press, 2018).

CHAPTER 20: THE GRAY

195 "Woman Divorces Her Husband": Jade Small, "Woman Divorces Her Husband While He Was Dying of Cancer," Secret Life of Mom, June 28, 2023, https://secretlifeofmom.com/woman-divorces-her-husband-while-he-was -dying-of-cancer/.

195 "The Ultimate Betrayal": Natalie Clarke, "The Ultimate Betrayal: I Cheated on My Dying Wife," *Daily Mail*, April 19, 2007, https://www.dailymail.co.uk /femail/article-449434/The-ultimate-betrayal-I-cheated-dying-wife.html.

195 "Cheating on a Sick Spouse": "Cheating on a Sick Spouse," ABC News, August 11, 2008, https://abcnews.go.com/Health/story?id=5559242&page=1.

CHAPTER 21: NOT WELL AT ALL

205 experiencing flashbacks and other PTSD symptoms: Judith Graham, "For Some Caregivers, the Trauma Lingers." *New York Times*, January 30, 2013,

https://newoldage.blogs.nytimes.com/2013/01/30/for-some-caregivers-the-trauma-lingers/.

205 how caregivers can cope with trauma symptoms: Barry J. Jacobs, "How to Handle Memories of Trauma," AARP, September 29, 2017, https://www.aarp.org/caregiving/life-balance/info-2017/ptsd-trauma-caregiver-support-fd.html.

205 documented prevalence of PTSD: Candice C. Johnson, et al., "Psychological Sequelae in Family Caregivers of Critically Ill Intensive Care Unit Patients. A Systematic Review," *Annals of the American Thoracic Society* 16, no. 7 (2019): 894–909, https://pubmed.ncbi.nlm.nih.gov/30950647/.

205 at a heightened risk for PTSD: Claudia Carmassi et al., "Risk and Protective Factors for PTSD in Caregivers of Adult Patients with Severe Medical Illnesses: A Systematic Review," *International Journal of Environmental Research and Public Health* 17, no. 16 (2020): 5888, https://doi.org/10.3390/ijerph17165888.

205 disability and caregiving even harder to talk about: Sami Schalk, *Black Disability Politics* (Duke University Press, 2022).

205 When PTSD affects people of color, it usually goes untreated: A. L. Roberts et al., "Race/Ethnic Differences in Exposure to Traumatic Events, Development of Post-Traumatic Stress Disorder, and Treatment-Seeking for Post-Traumatic Stress Disorder in the United States," *Psychological Medicine* 41, no. 1 (2011): 71–83, doi: 10.1017/S0033291710000401.

206 more caregivers than patients met the criteria for PTSD: Mutian Jia et al., "Post-Traumatic Stress Disorder Symptoms in Family Caregivers of Adult Patients with Acute Leukemia from a Dyadic Perspective," *Psycho-Oncology* 24, no. 12 (2015): 1754–60, https://doi.org/10.1002/pon.3851.

206 15 percent of caregivers for someone with cancer had experienced traumatic stress: Elizaveta Klekovkina et al., "Traumatic Stress in Caregivers of Adult Patients with Cancer: A Scoping Review," *Archives of Gerontology and Geriatrics Plus* 2, no. 2 (2025), 100141, https://doi.org/10.1016/j.aggp.2025.100141.

CHAPTER 22: THE SPLIT

207 "registers of evidence": Jenny Rice, *Awful Archives: Conspiracy Theory, Rhetoric, and Acts of Evidence* (Ohio State University Press, 2020).

208 "pivotal documents in the construction, experience, and rhetoric": Lauren Berlant, *The Queen of America Goes to Washington City: Essays on Sex and Citizenship* (Duke University Press Books, 1997).

208 this refuse, these leftovers, these scraps and ephemera: J. E. Muñoz, "Ephemera as Evidence: Introductory Notes to Queer Acts," *Women & Performance: A Journal of Feminist Theory* 8, no. 2 (1996): 5–16, https://doi.org/10.1080/07407709608571228.

210 Partition, *noun*: 1. The action: "partition," Merriam-Webster.com, https://www.merriam-webster.com/dictionary/partition.

210 Partition, *noun*: A partition: "Partition," TechTerms.com, https://techterms .com/definition/partition.

211 "uncanny alterations of consciousness": Judith L. Herman, *Trauma and Recovery: The Aftermath of Violence—from Domestic Abuse to Political Terror* (Basic Books, 1992).

211 "Traumatic events are extraordinary": Herman, *Trauma and Recovery*.

CONCLUSION: WHERE THERE IS A HISTORY THERE IS A FUTURE

222 different ways care collectives and care webs come to be: Akemi Nishida, *Just Care: Messy Entanglements of Disability, Dependency, and Desire* (Temple University Press, 2022).

223 *What are the best practices*: Leah Lakshmi Piepzna-Samarasinha, *Care Work: Dreaming Disability Justice* (Arsenal Pulp Press, 2018).

223 the state cannot be trusted to provide care: Ruth Wilson Gilmore, *Golden Gulag: Prisons, Surplus, Crisis, and Opposition in Globalizing California* (University of California Press, 2007).

223 caregivers of color utilize fewer "formal supports": Julian Chun-Chung Chow et al., "Types and Sources of Support Received by Family Caregivers of Older Adults from Diverse Racial and Ethnic Groups," *Journal of Ethnic and Cultural Diversity in Social Work* 19, no. 3 (2010): 175–94, https://doi.org /10.1080/15313204.2010.499318.

224 rely more on what are called "informal supports": Andrew E. Scharlach et al., "Cultural Attitudes and Caregiver Service Use," *Journal of Gerontological Social Work* 47, no. 1–2 (2006): 133–56, doi: 10.1300/J083v47n01_09.

224 "'cliff-hangers' that have yet to be resolved": Sins Invalid, *Skin, Tooth, and Bone: The Basis of Movement Is Our People* (Sins Invalid, 2019).

224 centered on the experience of white people: Jorge Matos Valldejuli, "The Racialized History of Disability Activism from the 'Willowbrooks of this World,'" *Activist History Review*, November 4, 2019, https://activisthistory .com/2019/11/04/the-racialized-history-of-disability-activism-from-the -willowbrooks-of-this-world/.

225 ease the eligibility burdens of means-tested programs: Beth Almeida, Isabela Salas-Betsch, and Christian E. Weller, "Updating SSI Would Improve the Economic Resilience of Low-Income Women," Center for American Progress, March 7, 2024, https://www.americanprogress.org/article/updating-ssi -would-improve-the-economic-resilience-of-low-income-women/.

225 universal healthcare: Alison P. Galvani et al., "Improving the Prognosis of Healthcare in the United States," *The Lancet* 395, no. 10223 (2020): 524–33, https://doi.org/10.1016/S0140-6736(19)33019-3.

225 better pay and working conditions for the care workers: Ai-jen Poo, *The Age of Dignity: Preparing for the Elder Boom in a Changing America* (New Press, 2016).

226 eliminating the Administration for Community Living: Julia Métraux, "RFK Jr. Moves to Close Administration for Community Living," *Mother Jones*,

March 28, 2025, https://www.motherjones.com/politics/2025/03/rfk-hhs-acl
-community-living-shutdown/.

226   threatening drastic cuts to Medicaid: Lena Marceno and Alyssa Llamas,
"Medicaid Cuts Could Jeopardize Access to Critical Long-Term Care Ser-
vices for People with Disabilities and Older Adults," Commonwealth Fund,
March 25, 2025, https://doi.org/10.26099/kcm3-at37.

226   seeking to weaken the protections against discrimination: "Trump's Executive Orders Target Accessibility and the Protections, Programs and Policies
That People with Disabilities Depend Upon," ADA Watch, February 17, 2025,
https://adawatch.org/2025/02/remember-the-a-in-deia-trumps-executive
-orders-target-accessibility-and-the-protections-programs-and-policies-that
-people-with-disabilities-depend-upon/.

226   takedown of DEIA programs: Executive Office of the President, "Executive
Order 14151: Ending Radical and Wasteful Government DEI Programs and
Preferencing," Federal Register, January 20, 2025, https://www.federalregister
.gov/documents/2025/01/29/2025–01953/ending-radical-and-wasteful
-government-dei-programs-and-preferencing.

226   Publicly funded infrastructure: Jina B. Kim, *Care at the End of the World*
(Duke University Press, 2025).

Index